If Cricket Is a Religion, Sachin Is God

Vijay Santhanam was born in Madras (now Chennai) and spent his schooldays in Madurai and Coimbatore. He graduated from the University of Roorkee—now Indian Institute of Technology, Roorkee—in 1986 and the Indian Institute of Management, Ahmedabad in 1988. He has wide ranging interests—writing, chess, films and travel—but one passion: cricket. He lives in Singapore.

Shyam Balasubramanian spent his childhood in Bombay (now Mumbai), a fifteen-minute walk from the Wankhede Stadium. He studied in the Cathedral & John Connon School, the Indian Institute of Technology, Kharagpur, and the Indian Institute of Management, Ahmedabad. His passions are writing, cricket and decoding game tactics across sports and this book offered the opportunity to indulge in all three areas. He now lives in London, an hour from his office but just fifteen minutes from Lord's.

If Cricket Is a Religion, Sachin Is God

VIJAY SANTHANAM
SHYAM BALASUBRAMANIAN

HarperCollins *Publishers* **India**

a joint venture with

New Delhi

First published in India in 2009 by
HarperCollins *Publishers* India
a joint venture with
The India Today Group

Copyright © Shyam Balasubramanian and Vijay Santhanam 2009

ISBN: 978-81-7223-821-6

2 4 6 8 10 9 7 5 3 1

Shyam Balasubramanian and Vijay Santhanam assert the moral
right to be identified as the authors of this work.

The views and opinions expressed in this book are the authors' own and the facts and
figures are as reported by them which have been verified to the extent possible, and the
publishers are not in any way liable for the same.

All rights reserved. No part of this publication may be reproduced,
stored in a retrieval system, or transmitted, in any form or by any means,
electronic, mechanical, photocopying, recording or otherwise,
without the prior permission of the publishers.

HarperCollins *Publishers*
A-53, Sector 57, Noida 201301, India
77-85 Fulham Palace Road, London W6 8JB, United Kingdom
Hazelton Lanes, 55 Avenue Road, Suite 2900, Toronto, Ontario M5R 3L2
and 1995 Markham Road, Scarborough, Ontario M1B 5M8, Canada
25 Ryde Road, Pymble, Sydney, NSW 2073, Australia
31 View Road, Glenfield, Auckland 10, New Zealand
10 East 53rd Street, New York NY 10022, USA

Typeset in 12/14 Perpetua
InoSoft Systems

Printed and bound at
Thomson Press (India) Ltd.

Ad majorem Dei gloriam
(To the greater glory of God)

CONTENTS

	Foreword: Harsha Bhogle	*ix*
1.	Fans and Fanatics	1
2.	The Wunderkind	9
3.	The Peak	23
4.	From Bodyline to Boringline	35
5.	The Fall: The Hidden Face of God	41
6.	The Resurrection	59
7.	The Case against Sachin Tendulkar	69
8.	The Case for Sachin Tendulkar	79
9.	The Player Viewpoint	125
10.	The Commentator Viewpoint	131
11.	Beyond Cricket: The Parallel Universe of Viswanathan Anand	139
12.	Beyond Sport: The Deification	155
13.	Beyond Debate	163
14.	And Then There Was One	171
	Epilogue: A Pilgrim's Progress	181
	Acknowledgements	195
	Photograph Acknowledgements	197

Foreword

Every day of his working life, Sachin Tendulkar has walked out on behalf of many million people. Of himself, too, but that is an expectation easily borne. But expectations of others? Of everyone else? People he doesn't know but who know him intimately? Students studying civics, housewives frustrated by tedium, executives facing a career block, pensioners searching for something to deliver them a smile? The unemployed, the impaired, the invalid?

If Sachin makes runs, a ray of light enters their lives, momentarily they let go of the present and rejoice till reality comes home again. But Sachin gives them *that* moment.

Unlike other heroes and earthly gods though, Sachin lives in the real world. There are no make-up men dabbing away, no retakes to fall back upon. There is no secretary writing his speeches, he can't make promises he doesn't intend to keep. And then there are bowlers trying to knock his stumps or his head off; many analysts and coaches searching for weaknesses and trying to plot his downfall; different bones and muscles crying out for relief. The only tougher job I know is saving a life or standing with a gun in Siachen; one noble, the other a tragic waste.

Often he delivers, occasionally he fails but the faithful rarely leave him. And that is because he carries intent with him, he tries every time. Some days, many days in fact, shots flow like Bhimsen Joshi or Pandit Jasraj, or dare I say Manna Dey, hitting the high notes. There are other days when he sheds cloak and crown, and scrapes. But he always tries. And he never snarls, never throws a tantrum on the field, never staggers drunk to his room. He is so easy to love!

And yet he is a measurable god. You cannot assign a percentage of success to the one who lives atop Mount Kailash or the one who ascended to heaven upon crucifixion. And that is what this book is about; measuring god. Vijay and Shyam are rational, analytical minds; people who measure and evaluate options and then take decisions that their organization trusts them with. It is such an approach that they have brought to this book.

I have discussed Sachin with them a couple of times. Sometimes they have agreed, with numbers to back them. At others they have disagreed, again with numbers. And that is why this book is a challenge. It is a rational response to an irrational emotion. And so you may occasionally disagree with its contents but you will have to do so with numbers.

Shyam and Vijay have dissected their god with devotion. This is their offering.

Meanwhile, Sachin Tendulkar remains a symbol of hope and joy.

—Harsha Bhogle

1
Fans and Fanatics

A book on cricket can begin with the rules of the game. It can begin with the institutions of cricket: Lord's, Eden Gardens, the Gabba, Sabina Park or *Wisden*. It can, more predictably, commence with the stars of the game. Or with the intermediaries: the writers, statisticians and bloggers who seek to interpret the esoteric in terms that are understandable.

We choose to start with the fans. For, in the absence of a fan base, the game of cricket would go the way of Indian hockey, a sport where the size of officialdom often exceeds the crowds in the stadium. To understand the game in all its aspects, it is important to understand those who watch it, even more than those who actually play it or make its rules.

We identify two broad categories of fans. There are those who typically appreciate the long form of the game—the five-day, all-white clothing variety—would applaud a good performance irrespective of the team, and seem to have an aesthetic attachment to the game. The Chepauk fan is an ideal example of this category.

Then there is the fanatic. For whom the event is a conflict between good and evil, to be won at any cost. The fanatics look upon it as a game about heroes and villains, with the heroes turning up for their team. The One Day Internationals (ODIs) target this audience. In this form of the game, it is significant that teams dress in different, more clannish forms of clothing.

To summarize: Test cricket targets the fan, ODIs the fanatic.

What about Twenty20? Twenty20 as a concept does a better job of targeting the fanatic. This is mostly because it does away with the ODI's middle overs (20–40), which to the fanatic are a drag. The Twenty20 format allows the fanatic to indulge in merriment, cheerleading and rabble-rousing, and of course does not have the dead phase between overs 20 and 40. So it's a slicker proposition. The addition of cheerleaders completes the symbolism: defeat the enemy, grab the loot, get the girl. During the first Indian Premier League (IPL), we could pick up the rallying cry of the fanatics, first disappointed by Delhi's qualification ahead of Bombay for the semifinals, and then enjoying Delhi's ignominious defeat in the semifinals. 'Sehwag ... go to Ranji', 'Sehwag ... go to Ranji', they jeered, and then 'Delhi ... what happened? Delhi ... what happened?'

Barracking the 'enemy' is as much a part of the fanatic experience as supporting your team.

So what has this got to do with religion?

The amazing thing is that the word 'religion' itself lacks a consistently agreed upon definition. We place before you a few options to consider.

The Oxford English Dictionary: 'Action or conduct indicating a belief in, reverence for, and desire to please a divine ruling power, the exercise or practice of rites and observances implying this ... a particular system of faith worship.' Or you could settle for Jawaharlal Nehru's definition, in the context of Hinduism in India, as religion being a way of life.

Meanwhile, Gwen Griffith-Dickson has noted that Sanskrit is a language that has no word for religion (it's not the only one, by the way; Hawaiian is another language that does not have a word for it). Timothy Fitzgerald's view of religion is quite pertinent here. He argues that the word 'religion' is not a genuine, cross-cultural category, but something imposed on different cultures: 'I propose that religious studies be rethought and represented as cultural studies, understood as the study of the institutions and the institutionalized values of specific societies, and the relation between those institutionalized values and the legitimation of power.'

So what does all this have to do with cricket?

If the word religion is just a word to describe a culture then there are many new cultures emerging which are getting more time and attention from people than conventional religions.

There is a footballing culture in the UK, where the weekend games are followed as enthusiastically as any sermon. There are 'the pundits', the commentators who seek to interpret the happenings on the football field to the faithful. And there are the performers on the field who are deified or demonized depending on which side of the fence you happen to sit and subject to whether the players you support answer your prayers. To hear the fans sing is to watch religion in action. You can scarcely listen to the Liverpool fans sing without your hair standing on end.

Similarly, there is a cricketing culture in the Indian subcontinent, which has shown itself capable of absorbing as much time as a fan or fanatic can throw at it. Every day, people sit transfixed by the drama occurring before them. Cricket first replaced traditional sport like hockey and football. Then it devoured weekends, with the traditional weekends with family being taken over by ODIs. Finally, it has taken over entertainment with Twenty20 cricket, which consumes time which would ordinarily have gone to hobbies, but more likely to TV serials or movies.

Like a religion, cricket has consumed other cultural options and traditions and stands ready to capture ever more. Nearly half a billion people are transfixed by the spectacle, pray for success and weep copiously when defeated.

If this is not religion, what is it? The opium of the masses? Well, that would make it a religion too.

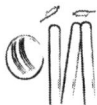

To come back to the subject of fans and fanatics, how are their attitudes different?

To address this, one has to delve into Raimon Pannikar, who has classified four types of attitudes towards religion. But where the religion of cricket is concerned, let us focus on three.

Fans are 'inclusivists'. They can see merit in the opposing team. They cannot while cheering for England or India not see the merit in a Shane Warne or an Abdul Qadir.

For the cricketing fanatic, his attitude is fundamentally 'exclusivist', which is to say, his team is simply the best and any failure of the team must come from causes other than the merits of the opposition. It could be the umpiring, the groundsman, match fixers or the fact that his own team was insufficiently motivated. But it cannot be because the other team was more skilful or stronger than his own.

What Twenty20 (thanks to multi-country leagues) is creating is a completely new religious attitude in the subcontinent—'interpenetration'—which implies that having opposing team players in 'my' team enriches my team and completes it. This form of acceptance that the other's 'faith' can enrich without challenging one's own is the future hope of cricket. In England the prevalence of international cricket players for many decades now has led to this inclusivist and interpenetrative attitude. This will happen in the subcontinent with the development of league cricket. While the fanatic will remain devoted to his team, which is inherent in his very nature and the reason why he follows the sport, the nationalist and conventionally religious reasons for supporting the team will decrease, resulting paradoxically, in something closer to a real fan.

Cricket is a way of life on the subcontinent. It consumes a disproportionate amount of people's time and energy for a normal sport. It has a subculture with codes of behaviour clearly defined, such as 'good' is playing for the team, 'evil' is playing for the self. It has a rule book and high priests (umpires) who interpret the book in real time. It promises a paradise on earth for those who deliver for the team and purgatory for those who cross the line, like fixing matches and slapping team-mates. It is a religion, and the players are at the centre of it, the demigods of the subculture.

While we have described cricket as a religion in a cultural sense, we hasten to add that at no point will there be made any analogy between the people who run cricket and those who seek to organize religion. For, any analysis into the inner workings of the International Cricket Council (ICC) or the Board of Control for Cricket in India (BCCI), or any other cricket board, can only reveal a mix of mundane bureaucrats and street-smart entrepreneurs.

For media companies, boards, and, of late, for the players, cricket has no purpose other than to entertain and to make money. But the game itself fortunately has ennobling characteristics and some (a small minority of) players also have the ability to uplift the game and the soul of fan and fanatic alike.

This upliftment could come about from a simple appreciation of skill or from an awe-inspiring display of sustained performance. But one suspects that any inquiry into matters concerning cricketing administration would swiftly convert even the most devoted fanatic into a cricket atheist. Perhaps it is best that, in the Indian context, only the Parliament is covered live and not any selection meeting. Transparency is fine when the inner workings are worthy of scrutiny. But the wheeling-dealing that goes on in matters of selection and the allotment of games to centres is best left unseen. Sporting bodies in a number of countries seem to reek of cronyism. A senior functionary on the Indian Hockey Federation, for example, allegedly offered selection to players on the basis of a bribe. Perhaps it is the bringing together of a noble game, unworthy functionaries and big money, which results in these unholy arrangements.

But every time there is a challenge to cricket—match-fixing, ball-tampering, or rebel leagues—the game manages to save itself. It could be through a superlative individual performance or a close game. The game has the capacity to cleanse itself through what it has to offer. When Indian cricket lost credibility after the match-fixing scandal, it was resurrected by the unforgettable home series against Australia in 2001. Similarly, when Australia was rocked by the diuretic scandal which put Warne out of the 2003 World Cup, the team responded with a spectacular performance to win the tournament without a single loss.

What does all this mean for the cricketer—the star of the game?

If you enjoy the adulation, there can be nothing better—at least while it lasts. If you don't, there can be nothing worse.

If you can be indifferent, there can be nothing better for your own long-term mental well-being.

Occasionally, the subcontinent throws up a Kapil Dev, Imran Khan, Sunil Gavaskar or Arjuna Ranatunga. Players admired by their team and countrymen, feared by their rivals, and, most importantly, men with an implicit sense of their own destiny. When Imran or Gavaskar came out to bowl or bat, defeat was the last thing on their mind. But many others, almost as talented, have wilted under the pressure and the high-calorie burden of initial success. That's what the pressure of fans and fanatics can do. It can turn a World Cup-winning hero one day into a nervous wreck in a few months. It can turn the talented into plodders and the incandescent into burnouts seeking redemption in part-time Bollywood roles.

Which is why comparisons between cricket and the Indian film industry, though often made, are quite superfluous. Apart from the apparent glamour, there's nothing in common. In films, while shooting, you have a small crew, a few hundred spectators at most and several retakes. In cricket, you have up to 100,000 people roaring in a stadium, up to 400 times that number watching the same game on television, and there are simply no retakes. The possibility of seizing the moment or, conversely, making a complete ass of yourself and bearing the consequences is far beyond anything possible in films.

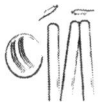

When Argentina played Italy in the 1990 World Cup in Italy, it was reported that fans of Napoli supported Maradona. If true, this is fascinating. Few sporting figures have the combination of charisma, spatial intelligence, talent, ball control, gift for controversy, or the political intent of a Maradona. Now take Maradona, and transplant him into an Indian context. Keep the talent, the charisma and the mass appeal. Subtract the controversy and replace the strident political overtones with a Buddha-like silence on any inappropriate issue.

What you would be left with is Sachin Tendulkar.

In this book we will seek to understand the career of Sachin Ramesh Tendulkar—the rise of the wunderkind, his peak, his dark phase and his resurrection. We will address the tough questions asked of him—through the lens of statistics. We will look at the criticism he is subjected to by Ian Chappell and Cricinfo among others. Numbers are not everything, but once one has framed and understood the match context, they are certainly stronger than opinions. We will compare him with his peers in both major forms of the game and present you with the data, so you can independently draw conclusions. The data are what they are, you be the judge.

While on the subject of data, there is an important point that the reader needs to note. All data and conclusions in the book till Chapter 13 are as of May 2008, when the manuscript was completed. We have added a few key highlights of the period June–December 2008 in Chapter 14.

2

The Wunderkind

From the outset, he could bat in the classical way. Coaches and contemporaries insist that he was not taught the game; it came from within, like an underground spring.

—PETER ROEBUCK

In 1986, there were four of us in a room in our engineering institute. Two were from Bihar and two from Bombay (now Bombay). One of the students from Bihar popped the all-important question that had been troubling most Indian cricket fans: 'What will happen to Indian cricket after Gavaskar retires? Who will carry the team?'

If 'After Nehru, who?' was the question that troubled the 1960s generation, the 'After Gavaskar' question was the one that occupied the minds of Indian cricket fans—at least till 1989.

The two of us from Bombay (C.R. Parmeswaran and Shyam Balasubramanian) answered simultaneously, 'Sachin Tendulkar.' And following the chorused answer probably smiled in an irritatingly knowing manner. I couldn't see the expression on my face, but the other guy looked smugly certain, so I'm pretty sure I would have looked the same.

The answer stumped the two Biharis—Arun Pandey and Sanjay Kumar—and one of them asked, 'Kaun Sachin?'

I clearly remember that moment, because the remarkable thing was that Sachin was only thirteen years old at that time. Yet the two of us who had been following Bombay cricket were 100 per cent certain about our answer.

For, in 1986, Tendulkar at the age of thirteen had already played in the Kanga league in Bombay. Nowadays, it is customary to hear people refer to the Kanga league almost dismissively: 'Oh that's Kanga league bowling.' But for any follower of Bombay cricket, the Kanga league was at the time a very big deal indeed as it was the nursery of Indian batting. For a thirteen-year-old to play in the Kanga league was incredible, as improbable as a Boris Becker winning Wimbledon at the age of seventeen.

The sheer insanity of our belief that a thirteen-year-old could carry the burden of Indian batting the way Gavaskar did (along with G.R. Viswanath) for nearly two decades did not strike us. Such is the suspension of logic and rationality when confronted by a wunderkind. (And before we proceed, let us clarify that when we say 'wunderkind' we refer to individuals who have a gift but who have a choice on whether or not to use it. I am not referring to the products of state-sponsored sporting farms like the erstwhile East Germany, which separate children from society at an early age and groom them to win empty steroid-tainted laurels for the state until the next batch from the farm arrives.)

There must have been something in the air that season which enabled these wunderkinds to defy the laws of men, and to write their own scripts. The 1985–86 sporting season was a glorious one for many reasons. Diego Maradona, another wunderkind-turned-man, took football to a plane it had probably never touched before and has equally probably never touched since. It was the season Boris Becker retained his Wimbledon title, which he had first won as a seventeen-year-old. Even more miraculously, the Indian cricket team won the Benson & Hedges World Championship of Cricket in Australia in an authoritative manner, without losing a single match, and even beating an Imran Khan-led Pakistan twice (an event staggering for its rarity).

Wunderkinds have this amazing ability to make grown men and women lose their sense of scepticism and rationality. There are sports where youth is an advantage—gymnastics and diving being just two of them. Cricket, especially if you happen to be a batsman, is not one of them. For a thirteen-year-old, a good length, or just short of a good length, ball is likely to be head high, the power to clear the infield is usually not there yet and the consequences of an injury are likely to be more severe. When more recently the leg-spinner Piyush Chawla made his debut against England at the age of seventeen, there was a banner in the crowd, '*Chawla doodh shood piyo bhai* (Chawla, go and drink some milk)', probably a reference as much to his age as to the seven-inch height advantage he conceded to the likes of Kevin Pietersen and Andrew Flintoff. Then, even if a cricketer survives this phase, he has to survive the easy money, fame and the things that go with it.

Sachin Tendulkar represents a discontinuity in Indian batting. For, till Tendulkar arrived, most Indian batsmen had been groomed to win by attritional cricket—the classical Bombay batting doctrine: give the first hour to the bowler and take the rest of the day from him. There were brief flashes where Sandeep Patil challenged that premise or Krishnamachari Srikkanth virtually invented hitting over the top in the first fifteen overs of an ODI (a strategy followed up with glee by the likes of Mark Greatbatch of New Zealand and Sanath Jayasuriya of Sri Lanka).

But on a consistent basis, in Tests and ODIs alike, no Indian batsman could sustain an attacking style of play where hitting through the line was the norm. Why Indian cricket has relied on the attritional style based on skill and not on a sporty, athletic style is worthy of deeper analysis.

Our pet theory on this is that cricket should not be a first and only sport, but a second one. Those who want to play cricket will be better equipped for the modern game with its emphasis on athleticism if they have played a more robust physical game before taking up cricket. At the very minimum they should have played another sport at least as seriously as cricket up to their teenage years. The physical foundation of a sportsman should be built by a more muscle-building sport like rugby, football or Aussie Rules, and then and only then should the player make a full-time transition to cricket. The success of Australia has much to do with its development of multi-sports players into cricketers. From Keith Miller to Ricky Ponting, Aussie Rules Football has built the muscle foundation on which skill can be topped. For England, Dennis Compton showed up for both Arsenal in football and England in cricket—a truly staggering achievement matched only to a slightly lesser degree by Ian Botham who managed to make it to Scunthorpe United apart from his phenomenal cricketing achievements. For the West Indies, Vivian Richards was a footballer for Antigua, and in the case of Pakistan, both Imran Khan and Wasim Akram have commented that they took to cricket rather late.

While Tendulkar did play tennis and table tennis, it was not at a national or state level, and very early on his single-minded focus was on cricket. Incidentally, his original intention was to be a fast bowler, which he was dissuaded from pursuing, on account of his height, by Dennis Lillee. His mentality, however, has remained that of a fast bowler and not of a traditional Bombay batsman for most of his career. The traditional mentality is that a rock-solid defence is the foundation of batting. When beaten the batsman lapses into defence mode like a tortoise retreating into its shell at the first sign of danger. The Tendulkar mentality is to show the bowler who the boss is by attacking early. If the bowler manages to beat the bat then counterattack to put him in his place. This mentality is like that of a fast bowler who reacts with an aggressive short ball when hit for a boundary.

In India, there is little space in big cities for more robust games. We believe that focus on cricket as a sole sport from an early age actually comes in the way of players developing a more robust physique. Some of our friends insist that genetics is the reason for Indian cricketers relying less on power and more on skill.

Then there is a case made for nutritional deficiencies. The socialist policies from 1950 to 1990 produced a nation of scarcities with ration shops and powdered milk. It was only after liberalization that nutrition became more widely available leading to a more robust post-1990s generation. Nevertheless, the physical evidence is that we produced several generations of portly, immobile cricketers, who were still able to compete, if not with success, then at least with distinction. Stunted by the inability to compete physically in terms of speed and strength, Indians converted the sport of cricket into a mind game like chess, by relying on spin, close-in catchers with lightning reflexes and batsmen who would wear down the opposition players by occupying the crease for long intervals of time, and then scoring when the bowlers were tired and the advantage of speed and power had eroded. As a game strategy, it was worthy of Sun Tzu. We are not sure if it was developed consciously or just happened as a matter of course, more probably the latter.

This was thus seen as the archetypal Indian style of play. Our greatest successes before Tendulkar came when we slowed the game down, not when we speeded it up. Away wins in West

Indies and England in the 1970s under Ajit Wadekar came from spin and the technical correctness of Gavaskar and Dilip Sardesai. India's World Cup win in 1983 came from the ability of dibbly-dobbly bowlers to confuse batsmen with late swing. And the Benson & Hedges success in 1985 came from early swing from Kapil Dev, Madan Lal and Roger Binny followed by spinners Ravi Shastri and L. Sivaramakrishnan choking opposing batsmen in the middle overs, so we were never chasing high targets. But it is not unique to cricket or India to slow a game down to win it when the other side has a physical advantage. For example, in 1975, Arthur Ashe won the Wimbledon final against a younger, stronger Jimmy Connors by slowing down the pace of the game with 'junk' balls. Jimmy Connors liked to hit the ball on the rise—early and hard. So Ashe fed him plenty of lobs and soft drop shots so that there was less pace for Connors to hit his famed powerful ground strokes.

Recently, with improving nutritional standards, the Indian cricket team is producing monster hitters like a Yuvraj Singh or a Mahendra Dhoni, and the slow-burning Indian school of attritional cricket has vanished somewhat, as the search for the next fast bowler or power hitter is proving easier than the search for a great spinner or a batsman who can occupy the crease in Tests.

Finally, there is the question of whether our selectors earlier were looking beyond the big cities. If in those days there was a small-town equivalent of Dhoni, our selectorial search engine would probably have missed him. The economic rise of small-town India (known as Bunty and Babli towns after a popular Bollywood movie) has resulted in the selection of a whole new generation of cricketers hailing from outside the Bombay–Delhi–Calcutta–Bangalore–Hyderabad–Madras corridor. When people sometimes ask why a billion people can't produce a winning cricket team, it is useful to remind them that up until the post-1990 economic liberalization programme, there were only forty million middle-class households; of these only half were in the cities, which had a powerful say in selection, and even among these cities, sporting activity was actively discouraged as being a distraction which would come in the way of securing a job.

Be all that as it may, we were as a cricketing nation accustomed to elegant, skill-based batsmen, who would rely on precision, skill and placement to accumulate runs. Sachin broke with tradition, to hit the ball fearlessly in the air, give the fastest and best bowlers the charge and carry a heavy bat which was till then the preserve of big West Indians like Clive Lloyd.

In summary, our first theory is that pursuing just cricket alone as a sport is not necessarily the best way to develop a physique suited to the demands of the modern game. On that count, for Sachin to have primarily been a cricketer and then develop as a robust hitter is indeed noteworthy. Kapil Dev was another discontinuity for Indian cricket in terms of bowling, batting and fielding—and he played many other forms of sport, not just cricket. His contribution to Indian cricket has not been analysed in this book, only because it would have made it twice as long to read. His intention to attack and bowl fast mirrors Sachin's desire to attack and score quickly in all forms of the game. But even Kapil Dev was allowed the luxury of turning nineteen, before being thrown into the big league, which, while still very young in the context of 1970s cricket, did not border on the improbability of a sixteen-year-old batsman in an away tour to Pakistan.

The second theory is that Sachin's developing years were when creative (rather than technical) players like Maradona, Richards and John McEnroe dominated sport. This is significant given that the Bombay school of batting had till then produced several technicians but few out-of-the-box players. Mastery of technique, like academic success, was to be admired and almost an end in itself. Several Indian batsmen, especially from Bombay, have fallen into the trap of developing the perfect technique. The Indian education system is based on being able to successfully reproduce correct answers rather than invent new ones. It comes as no surprise therefore that replicating successful techniques, and not innovating new shots, is regarded as admirable by most Indian coaches. Sachin's breakthrough arose from the fact that he probably realized by looking at other sports that technique was merely a means to an end; true mastery lay in going beyond technique. By treating batsmanship more creatively, he was not only able to improve the scoring rate compared to the technically correct—something of immense significance in the one-day era—but has also been able to retain his interest in the game and that of the spectators in *his* game for over two decades. It comes as no surprise therefore that he rates Maradona and McEnroe among his favourite sportsmen. People who followed Bombay cricket and saw the curly-headed youngster could clearly see that his role models were as much from outside cricket as from it. There probably will be several arguments against this and a case can be made that Sachin's coach, Ramakant Achrekar, should be given credit for letting his natural game develop. We counter that on the ground that his natural game is not the natural game of almost all Indian batsmen who preceded him. It is his own interpretation of Maradona, McEnroe and Richards. No doubt Achrekar deserves full credit for Tendulkar's defensive technique, but his burning desire to attack and dominate the bowling does not come from a coach or a coaching manual. This is intrinsic to how the cricketer wants to achieve success. There has always been an element of schoolboy cheekiness in Tendulkar's batting when he is in form.

Wunderkinds do not get discovered. They do not score the usual well-constructed 40 or 50, get discovered by a mentor, refine their technique, get dropped, come back and so on. They simply announce themselves as the future.

In February 1988, playing for Sharadashram School against St Xavier's High School in the Harris Shield semifinal, Tendulkar, aged fifteen, and his classmate Vinod Kambli went on to amass a record unbeaten stand of 664 with Tendulkar scoring 326 and Kambli 349. Their impishness in refusing to listen to their coach, in refusing to declare, etc., is well documented. But there is a literary precedent to this. Mike (in P.G. Wodehouse's celebrated schoolboy cricket novel *Mike and Psmith*) played a similar innings of 277 not out with his team refusing to declare as they enjoyed a schoolboy prank. In many ways, that Tendulkar–Kambli partnership had the authority and cheek of schoolboy heroes in a novel.

It is reasonably well known that in the next three years, Tendulkar was to score centuries on debut in the Ranji, Irani and Duleep trophies. To put things in context, this is akin to a fifteen-year-old footballer scoring a goal in his first appearance in each of the following: the English Premiership, FA Cup and Carling Cup. It is so absurd that it borders on the fictional. In this case, it is true. Wunderkinds write their own script.

At this stage, let's dwell briefly on England captain Mike Gatting. Gatting was a popular figure among Indian crowds, as portly figures tend to be. Now, Gatting was a pugnacious cricketer with a couple of stellar achievements—scoring 575 runs at an average of 95 in an away series win in India in 1984–85 and winning an Ashes series in Australia as captain in 1986–87. However, he also has the unfortunate distinction of facing two of the most brutal balls in cricket history. The first, from Malcolm Marshall (Kingston, 1986), would have been as pleasant as being punched by Mike Tyson and having your nasal bone smashed into your brain. The second, from Shane Warne (Manchester, 1993), would begin an era of Australian mental dominance of the Ashes; it became clear from that one ball that facing Warne was going to be as much fun as solving Sudoku problems with 50,000 people watching.

The significance of the first of the Gatting balls was that it established firmly that a tour to the West Indies was a health hazard for batsmen. In 1989, India was to visit the West Indies for a tour which was remarkable not for what happened (India lost 3–0) but for what could have happened, because Tendulkar, aged sixteen then, was apparently very keen to go to test himself against Marshall, Ambrose, Walsh and Bishop. He was not allowed to go and we will never know whether this decision was a sensible one or an opportunity lost. The series against Pakistan followed soon after, against a bowling attack of Imran Khan, Wasim Akram and Waqar Younis. This was regarded as being only marginally less physically threatening than the West Indies. Moreover, Pakistan had Abdul Qadir who, many Pakistan fans say to this day, would have achieved as much as Warne if he had been supported by the selectors. Imran had slowed down from his unplayable 1982 form but Waqar and Wasim were young, fit and quick.

The rest is history. Tendulkar got one on his nose from Waqar and, a bloody interlude later, proceeded to hit the next ball for a boundary, thereby establishing that he had the courage and temperament for Test cricket. In a separate incident, in a twenty-over exhibition match in Peshawar, Tendulkar hit 53 in eighteen balls nearly taking India to a win. Tendulkar had hit Mushtaq Ahmed for a couple of sixers, when he was challenged by Qadir, 'Why are you only hitting the kid? Hit me too.' His response was 28 runs in Qadir's next over (6, 0, 4, 6, 6, 6). These two moments, where challenge was met with immediate response, showed the heart of a fast bowler hidden in a batsman.

The point being made is that it is one thing to be able to play the best bowlers in the world, but it is quite another thing to want to play them, and still another to do so at the age of sixteen.

The period from Tendulkar's debut through to his twentieth birthday in 1993 is extremely significant. The bald statistics show that he played 25 Tests and scored 1522 runs at an average of 44.76 with five centuries and eight half-centuries. Significantly, these centuries were against Australia (Perth and Sydney), South Africa (Johannesburg) and England (Manchester and Bombay), i.e., four out of the five tons were made away. In Manchester, he saved the game, when India, set 408 in the fourth innings, managed to hold out for a draw with 343/6, mainly due to an unbeaten 119 from Tendulkar. A century in Perth (114) followed a special hundred in Sydney against an excellent Australian pace attack. The Sydney innings was rated by Richie Benaud as one of the finest, if not the finest, played on Australian soil by a non-Australian. (Later, in 1996, we heard of Tendulkar being compared to Bradman—by Bradman himself in a comment to his wife.) During that period, batting in the middle order in ODIs, he scored 1520 runs in 56 matches at an average of 32.34. The decision to make him open hadn't been taken yet and, batting between slots four and six, his position was more that of a utility ODI player.

However, he had already begun to accumulate a body of work—by his twentieth birthday he had saved an away Test in England, played arguably the best Test innings in Australia and had become the lead batsman in the Indian team. In comparison, by the age of twenty, his peers among the modern Test match greats—Brian Lara, Ricky Ponting, Matthew Hayden, Adam Gilchrist, Rahul Dravid and Steve Waugh—had not played a single Test or ODI.

Tendulkar had in effect leapfrogged straight from club to international arena at the highest level with just a minor detour through first-class cricket. Considering the preparation that goes into making a Test player in terms of technique, confidence and style, this is very hard to conceive. This is what being a wunderkind is all about—suspension of the normal laws of cricketing development. To succeed young is one thing, to survive the spoils of success another.

Curiously, the real star of Tendulkar's debut Test series was Sanjay Manjrekar. A traditional Bombay cricketer, Sanjay is the son of the highly respected Vijay Manjrekar, a Test player of the 1950s and '60s, and was therefore blue blood as far as Indian cricket is concerned. Sanjay possibly had the best defensive technique since Gavaskar and till the arrival of Dravid. If batting had only been about defence, perhaps this book would have been about Manjrekar. Sanjay Manjrekar scored 569 runs at an average of 94.83 in Tendulkar's debut series and was the primary reason why India held Pakistan to an honourable draw. He would have been justified in thinking that the mantle of Indian cricket was to pass to him. But in just a few series, notably away in England (1990) and Australia (1991–92), the mantle was to pass swiftly to the teenaged Tendulkar. Manjrekar went on to have a moderately successful if unspectacular Test career (2043 runs in 37 Tests at an average of 37.14), and a more successful career as a commentator and writer. Nobody other than Manjrekar will know the reason why, in later years, he would return as Tendulkar's nemesis and chief critic along with Ian Chappell.

In Indian cricket, success does not just breed several fathers, but millions of fans and several demanding critics. Surviving both the adulation and the criticism takes a certain temperament, which only very few in Indian cricket have possessed.

3

The Peak

We'd been privileged to have a free, up close and personal lesson in how to pulverize an attack on a turning wicket.

—STEVE WAUGH on Sachin's 155 not out at Madras, March 1998, in *Out of My Comfort Zone*

When faced with a mountain range sometimes one can easily identify 'The Peak' as in the case of Mount Everest in the Himalayas. For most sportspersons, this peak normally lasts a year or two. In contrast, Sachin ruled for close to a dozen years at his peak. And different experts think of different years as his peak. This is understandable—we have the records that explain why.

But there is an important factor which affected Sachin's records that we need to consider. Sachin's rise coincided with one of India's most shameful eras in international cricket. This was the period when the match-fixing scandal broke over the Indian landscape and it singed the Indian team like no other. A number of Indian players were suspected to have made deals with bookies to influence match results and were banned. In effect, it may not be an exaggeration to say that for some time in the 1990s, Sachin had to play not only against the opposition but also against some team members bent on selling the team short. It must have had a dampening effect on Sachin, someone who takes obvious pride in his game. When even the most senior batsman could be playing with non-cricketing considerations in mind, how difficult it must have been for a young player like Sachin to retain his enthusiasm for the game. And not just retain it, but play it with passion and pride through that difficult decade and beyond. Sachin's dozen years at the peak were much more extraordinary because of the incredibly challenging team context.

To pick a particular year is tough; but we will try. In the earlier chapter we covered Sachin as a teen; now we start at age twenty, in the year 1993 when, almost on cue, Sachin touched a peak. Table I demonstrates his performance in the year.

Table I: Sachin in Tests and ODIs, 1993

Format	Matches	Runs	Average	Strike Rate	Centuries	Fifties	High Points
Tests	8	640	91	48	2	5	India beat England (home) 3-0; India beat Sri Lanka (away) 1-0
ODIs	18	319	25	73	0	1	Last over in Hero Trophy semifinals

It is instructive to have a look at his run of scores in the Test matches he played in the year: 73 vs South Africa in Cape Town, 50 and 9 not out vs England in Calcutta, 165 vs England in Madras, 78 vs England in Bombay, 62 vs Zimbabwe in Delhi, 28 and 104 not out vs Sri Lanka in Colombo (SSC) and 71 vs Sri Lanka in Colombo (PSS). In effect he notched up a score over fifty in every Test he played in the year.

But 1993 heralded only the beginning of Sachin's peak. Actually, his ODI record in 1993 was ordinary despite his semifinal heroics at the Hero Cup, which helped India win against overwhelming odds. More importantly, it showed that he was willing to take personal risks for the sake of the team's cause. South Africa started the final over with 3 wickets in hand and needing 6 runs to win. Sachin managed to choke the batsmen so much that they scored only 3 runs, and two batsmen got run out too! According to Vaibhav Purandare's biography of Sachin (quoting Ajit Wadekar, who was the coach then), Wadekar sent a message to Azhar (who was the captain) that Kapil, the most experienced bowler, should bowl the last over. As Azhar, Kapil and Sachin were debating, Sachin grabbed the ball and said, 'I will bowl.' This despite the fact that Sachin had not bowled earlier in the match. Clearly, at the age of twenty, he had matured, was bold and showed leadership.

Interestingly, 1993 marked Vinod Kambli's year of triumph. As is very well known, Sachin was Kambli's close friend in school and they had put on a world-record unbroken 664-run partnership in a school match. They toyed with England to help India register its first 3-0 Test series win ever, before going on to help India win a Test series in Sri Lanka too.

Perhaps we need to talk about Kambli to understand Sachin better. Most people at the time thought that Kambli was as talented as Sachin. Let us analyse some of Kambli's figures. In terms of the number of innings played to score the first 1000 Test runs in one's career, Kambli comes fifth; this great start in Test matches was driven by two double centuries and two centuries in his first seven Tests! The list has some amazing names in it: H. Sutcliffe (England; 12 innings), E.D. Weekes (West Indies; 12 innings), D.G. Bradman (Australia; 13 innings), R.N. Harvey (Australia; 14 innings), V.G. Kambli (India; 14 innings), L. Hutton (England; 16 innings), F.M.M. Worrell (West Indies; 16 innings), L.G. Rowe (West Indies; 16 innings), G.A. Headley (West Indies; 17 innings) and S.G.

Barnes (England; 17 innings). In contrast, Sachin took 28 innings to complete 1000 runs in Tests.

Almost all of these batsmen are regarded as some of the finest exponents of their art. All of them went on to score runs by the thousands. Tendulkar is getting close to 12,000. Kambli, however, failed to add another thousand to his first. In fact, he went on to make only 84 more Test runs, for a career aggregate of 1084 runs. So what happened to Tendulkar's partner in that 664-run partnership? What happened to the man who is the fifth fastest to make 1000 runs in Test cricket when Sachin is not even in the top fifty in that list?

In a lecture at IIM, Ahmedabad, Harsha Bhogle once spoke about 'excellence'. He talked about Sachin's dedication and discipline. He pointed out that Sachin once played cricket for over fifty days continually. For Tendulkar, cricket is his food, his whole life and soul. Talent does not automatically translate into excellence. Unlike Sachin, Kambli was probably distracted and was not dedicated enough. Thankfully, Sachin never lost focus. Continuing the debate on his peak, let us go on to the next year, 1994.

Table II: Sachin in Tests and ODIs, 1994

Format	Matches	Runs	Average	Strike Rate	Centuries	Fifties	High Points
Tests	7	700	70.00	59.37	2	3	India beat SL 3-0, by margins of an innings
ODIs	25	1089	47.34	88.60	3	9	Sachin the opener!

His run of scores in the Test matches he played in the year reveals a player at his peak: 142 vs Sri Lanka in Lucknow, 96 vs Sri Lanka in Bangalore, 6 vs Sri Lanka in Ahmedabad; 43 and 11 not out vs New Zealand in Hamilton, 34 and 85 vs West Indies in Bombay; 179 and 54 vs West Indies in Nagpur, and 40 and 10 vs West Indies in Mohali.

Equally importantly, on 27 March 1994, Sachin was sent to open against New Zealand in an ODI. He made 82 runs off merely 49 balls (strike rate 167), and the rest is history. With more than 1000 ODI runs, three centuries (against Australia, New Zealand and West Indies) and nine fifties at an average of 47 and a strike-rate of 89 to add to his Test record for the year, can we conclude that Sachin was at his peak? Not yet, we say.

Ravi Shastri, a celebrated cricketer and now a commentator, thinks that 1996–97 was Sachin's peak period. We can easily understand why. The World Cup 1996 was a Sachin show all the way: 127 not out vs Kenya, 70 vs West Indies, 90 vs Australia, 137 vs Sri Lanka, 3 vs Zimbabwe, 31 vs Pakistan, and 65 vs Sri Lanka. Now examine the full year's data:

Table III: Sachin in Tests and ODIs, 1996

Format	Matches	Runs	Average	Strike Rate	Centuries	Fifties	High Points
Tests	8	623	41.53	48.78	2	2	'Lone ranger' in the England series: e.g., 122 (of India's 219) in Edgbaston

Continued

Format	Matches	Runs	Average	Strike Rate	Centuries	Fifties	High Points
ODIs	32	1611	53.70	82.44	6	9	Record total runs in a World Cup!

As is clear from Table III, Sachin's ODI record during the year was phenomenal. While his Test record in 1996 suggests that he was not exactly at his peak, the quality of innings and the context in which they were played should be taken into account: 24 and 122 versus England in Birmingham, 177 and 74 versus England in Nottingham, and 61 and 36 versus South Africa in Kanpur which helped India win a Test series. Now let us look at the data for 1997 to further verify Shastri's assessment.

Table IV: Sachin in Tests and ODIs, 1997

Format	Matches	Runs	Average	Strike Rate	Centuries	Fifties	High Points
Tests	12	1000	62.50	50.78	4	3	All three fifties were scores in excess of 80
ODIs	39	1011	30.63	84.95	2	5	-

As far as Test matches go, 1997 was indeed one of the best years for Sachin. Not just the numbers (which are great) but also the kind of innings he played—for example the 169 in Cape Town. After the disaster of the earlier Test (where India had been shot out for 100 and 66 in the two innings), the team was in deep trouble at 58 for 5; a great partnership between Sachin (169) and Azhar (115) helped India reach a reasonable total though we lost the game. But in ODIs, even though he scored 1000 runs, this was not a great year for Sachin.

So in effect, in these two years, he had a good Test run in one and a good ODI run in the other. Perhaps Shastri correctly combines the two years and arrives at the conclusion that 1996–97 was Sachin's peak year. In 1997, *Wisden* awarded Sachin its 'Cricketer of the Year' award. It's tempting to put that down as the defining moment of a player's peak period, but the story isn't over yet. Far from it.

In 1999, Sachin was prolific in Test matches with some epic innings as a lone ranger against the best (116 and 52 in Melbourne against Australia and then 136 in the fourth innings against archrival Pakistan in Madras) besides scoring heavily against Sri Lanka and New Zealand.

Table V: Sachin in Tests and ODIs, 1999

Format	Matches	Runs	Average	Strike Rate	Centuries	Fifties	High Points
Tests	10	1088	68.00	56.43	5	4	The Lone Ranger
ODIs	22	843	42.15	88.64	3	1	Played for India soon after his father's death, dedicated his 140 not out vs Kenya to him

However, his ODI form was nothing to write home about. Of course, for anyone else, an average of 42 with close to a thousand runs and three centuries would have been a peak performance, but Sachin had set higher standards. And it is his relatively below-par performance in the ODIs that prevents 1999 from being a peak year for Sachin.

A new millennium dawned; so did a new era in Indian cricket. Sourav Ganguly became captain (he would go on to become the most successful Test captain in Indian cricket), the team became stronger (especially in batting, where India at this point seemed to have an embarrassment of riches in Rahul Dravid, V.V.S. Laxman and Ganguly all playing at their best), and the doubts about whether a player was playing for India or for the bookies lessened. In short, though Sachin's peak might have passed (or did it?), at least his team members were playing with him. In 2000, Sachin was playing almost at his peak. But many of his Tests in the year were against weak teams, so we will move to 2001 (Table VI).

Table VI: Sachin in Tests and ODIs, 2001

Format	Matches	Runs	Average	Strike Rate	Centuries	Fifties	High Points
Tests	10	1003	62.68	57.15	3	6	Important contribution to a series win vs Australia
ODIs	17	904	69.53	91.31	4	3	Centuries against four different opponents

Sachin's exploits in Test matches in 2001 are worth detailing. Against Australia at home: 76 and 65 in Bombay, 10 and 10 in Calcutta (this was the famous Indian victory at Eden Gardens, Calcutta, after following-on, which stopped the Australian juggernaut, the Test justifiably famous for the heroics of Laxman, Dravid and Harbhajan), and 126 and 17 in Madras. Against Zimbabwe: 74 and 36 not out in Bulawayo (first Test win for India in Zimbabwe), 20 and 69 in Harare. Against South Africa: 155 and 15 in Bloemfontein, 1 and 22 not out in Port Elizabeth. Against England: 88 in Mohali, 103 and 26 in Ahmedabad, and 90 in Bangalore. His ODI centuries in this year were against Australia, West Indies and South Africa, besides Kenya. One could argue that 2001, going by the statistics, was Sachin's peak. In the year of the Calcutta miracle, Sachin 'quietly' made nearly 2000 runs, with seven centuries and nine fifties at an average above 60 in both Tests and ODI. Yet we still think he has done better in another year! That says a lot. On that note, let us look at 2002:

Table VII: Sachin in Tests and ODIs, 2002

Format	Matches	Runs	Average	Strike Rate	Centuries	Fifties	High Points
Tests	16	1392	55.68	54.20	4	5	Centuries with India winning in WI and England
ODIs	20	741	52.92	87.48	2	3	The road to the final at Lord's

Wisden has written eloquently about Sachin's second innings 176 against West Indies in Calcutta as one of the finest. After conceding a 139-run lead India was placed in a tough situation (11 for 2) when Sachin walked in. At 87 for 4, India was in real danger of losing the Test. Sachin in Laxman's company (154 not out) saved the game. These are the stats. Sachin's 176 was a real exhibition of defence (when needed) and offence with an overall strike rate of 59.

In 2002, Sachin made another 176 versus Zimbabwe, and then a winning century (117) in West Indies and another (193) in England. In ODIs, people remember that India won the NatWest series (played between India, England and Sri Lanka) with a memorable display in the finals. Chasing 325 runs to win, young Turks Yuvraj Singh and Mohammad Kaif took India to a victory that at one point, with India reeling at 146 for 5, looked improbable. But what most people forget is that it was Sachin's 105 not out against England in Chester-le-Street and 113 against Sri Lanka in Bristol that took India to the final! Was 2002 his peak or do we move on? Reluctantly, we move on!

Let us focus on the period from World Cup 2003 to the Pakistan series (first half of 2004). Sachin was the Man of the Series at the World Cup with knocks of 52 vs Netherlands, 36 vs Australia, 81 vs Zimbabwe, 152 v Namibia, 50 vs England, 98 vs Pakistan, 5 vs Kenya, 97 vs Sri Lanka, 15 vs New Zealand, 83 vs Kenya and 4 vs Australia (total 673 runs, still a record). He won the Man of the Series in the triangular competition at home (against Australia and New Zealand) with centuries against each; scored 241 not out and 60 not out in the Test at Sydney against Australia, and piled up 194 not out in Multan (helping India to win its first Test series in Pakistan). Great year indeed, but not Sachin's best!

This is the crux.

For close to a dozen years (1993 to 2003–04), almost every year was memorable and could be argued as 'Sachin's Best' across Test matches and ODIs, whether other team members were in form or not, even if the openers were underperforming, whether he was captain or not, whether India won or lost, whether at home or away against various opponents. This is the kind of extraordinary consistency that fans and cricket followers have got used to expecting from Sachin. A dozen years at the peak, year after year, series after series, living up to the expectations of a billion cricket-crazy people. Sometimes when there are many peaks close to each other, it all looks a little flat.

And yes. We almost forgot (not really!) the Peak. We rate 1998 as Sachin's best year, the 'peak of peaks' as we could like to call it. Sometimes, the statistics say everything. Just relish Sachin's 1998!

Table VIII: Sachin in Tests and ODIs, 1998

Format	Matches	Runs	Average	Strike Rate	Centuries	Fifties	High Points
Tests	5	647	80.87	75.40	3	1	First-ever Test series win vs Australia at full strength
ODIs	34	1894	65.31	102.15	9	7	World record runs in a year. The famous 'desert storm' innings. Six final wins against five opponents with four centuries and an average of 155.5.

4

From Bodyline to Boringline

Whatever he [Nasser Hussain] did was within the regulations of the game—there was no stage where he broke any laws. He was a great tactician.

—SACHIN TENDULKAR quoted on Nasser Hussain

There are perhaps only two occasions in the history of cricket when an entire team strategy was based around stopping one man. The first instance was known as Bodyline, and the second could be called Boringline.

Let us look at the protagonists, Douglas Jardine and Nasser Hussain. On paper, they could not have been more different. Jardine, the son of a barrister, was educated at Winchester College, which, as Christopher Douglas's riveting biography, *Douglas Jardine: Spartan Cricketer*, put it, was dedicated to 'producing young gentlemen with the minds of philosophers and the bodies of Olympians'. Boys were woken up at 6.30 in the morning, had to bathe in cold water (even though hot water was available) and then, if they 'survived', study Greek and Latin. Nasser Hussain was part of a first generation of immigrants into the UK from India, who was moulded into becoming a cricketer and then captain by an ambitious father Joe (Jawad) Hussain. And Forest School was a different world from Winchester.

But both had some intriguing things in common. One, an India connection—both were born in India—Jardine in Bombay and Nasser in Madras. Two, both were captains of England, called upon to turn around weak teams. Three, both were fully capable of pushing the game to the limits of what the rules would permit. And both used bowling tactics which were unconventional, to say the least, to control a batsman they did not have a conventional answer to.

Jardine was aware that in 1930, Bradman had scored 974 runs in just five Tests at an average of 139.14. Clearly, he was looking for some way to control Bradman. Otherwise, the tour of Australia promised to be a long, hot leather hunt. Similarly, Nasser Hussain would have been painfully aware that the last time England played India in India in 1992–93, Tendulkar had scored 302 runs in just three Tests at an average of 100.66, and India had won the series 3-0.

How Bodyline worked was very simple. Four to six fielders in the leg trap with medium-fast bowlers bowling short. But Jardine had one trump card up his sleeve, Harold Larwood, who was capable of making the ball rear at around 90 mph from a conventional length. This left the batsman three options: fend, hook or get hit. With two fielders placed in the deep, hooking was risky. Fending with the close-in leg-side field was even less attractive. The third option was to get hit, which in an era lacking helmets and rudimentary protective equipment was suicidal.

Boringline worked on an equally simple mechanism. To quote Nasser, 'I wanted [Matthew] Hoggard to bowl a yard outside off-stump to him [Tendulkar] with an 8–1 field. I wanted Freddie Flintoff to come round the wicket to him every now and then and try to hit him in the ribs, with two men out on the hook and a short leg to unsettle him.' And then there was the matter of the left-arm spinner Ashley Giles bowling into the rough wide outside the leg-stump—in one controversial spell for 202 out of 204 balls.

In the tour matches, England had tested the strategy—just as they had done seventy years earlier. In his BBC Sport Online column earlier in the tour, Richard Johnson wrote, 'The positive for the bowlers was that they're working out their gameplans more clearly.' This was after the warm-up match against India-A. 'At one point, Matthew Hoggard was bowling to a field with nine men on the off side, putting it a little wider outside off stump. On a wicket so flat you have to look for ways to get wickets and it worked as they became frustrated with the blanket coverage and got a few edges.'

Responding to the criticism, Johnson later wrote, 'And there lies the reality as far as England is concerned. Without Darren Gough and Andrew Caddick, and on flat pitches—at least while India is batting—there is nothing to be gained from attacking at all times. Imagine—and John Wright please take note here—India without Harbhajan Singh and Anil Kumble. What tactics would Iqbal Siddiqui and Tinu Yohannan have employed in the first Test?'

But of course he missed a key point.

Andrew Flintoff and Matthew Hoggard were hardly Yohannan and Siddiqui, even accounting for the fact that Flintoff had not yet matured into the complete fast bowler he is today. The fundamental flaw in the theory was that England didn't stand a chance to win with the option. England had given up the possibility of getting Tendulkar out conventionally even before bowling a ball. In Hussain's own words, 'I think it was totally unfair and simplistic to call it a negative tactic. What did people expect us to do? Just lob it up to Sachin and then see him smack our inexperienced attack all over the place?'

This is not any captain speaking. This is probably one of the best captains England has ever produced. Reduced to having two good bowlers (they would become very, very good in a few years' time) bowl wide balls.

But that is the kind of desperation that Tendulkar can induce in an opposition.

Tendulkar scored 307 runs in the three-Test series at an average of 76.75. Nasser Hussain derived satisfaction in that he had cut his scoring rate down and kept the series margin to 1-0 compared to 3-0 in 1993.

Although we rate Nasser Hussain as one of the best Test captains we have seen, we feel that as a captain he underrated Flintoff, the bowler. He was so distraught about losing Caddick and Gough, that it did not cross his mind that perhaps someone even better could have stepped up. He missed the big picture, which was that he had young fast bowlers who could become better bowlers than Gough and Caddick. He looked at the India series more as a 'holding' series where he had to minimize damage because he had B-grade bowlers. He simply did not have the foresight to see what would become a statistical fact: these B graders were more talented than the A set.

This series was especially significant from the perspective of Tendulkar's batting evolution. After this series, one could sense that Tendulkar had become a lot more efficient and professional in his approach. That sense of cricket as pure entertainment had passed, and he had honed his batting to become even more efficient, with a ruthless dedication to scoring as many runs with as few risks as possible. In other words, he realized the price others were putting on his wicket, and started putting the same price on it. The Tendulkar before Boringline would neither have batted ten hours in Sydney for 241 not out nor played Ryan Sidebottom defensively for nine overs (in the 2007 series). But after Boringline, Tendulkar would also do what it took to win—he would adapt his style to the opponent's strategy; he would play exactly in the manner that they did not want him to. He would not be the Tendulkar you set your plans for; he would be the Tendulkar you could not have plans for.

Typically a batsman has a favourite scoring area. Batsmen are at times classified as predominantly leg-side or predominantly off-side players. After this series, Tendulkar developed into a complete batsman, one who could adopt different styles according to the bowler and the conditions. This increased his options whilst decreasing those of the opposition's. It also made him play any role the team required him to: hit a bowler off length, or see off in a defensive vein a particularly testing spell. It increased his understanding of batsmanship and his own usefulness to the team.

5
The Fall
The Hidden Face of God

A walking wicket.

—**ANONYMOUS comment on Sachin's form in 2006, quoted by John Stern, editor of** *The Wisden Cricketer* **in Cricinfo**

We are not superstitious. But we believe in the science of probabilities. And the study of the careers of many of the best batsmen cricket has produced over the last forty years has led us to conclude that sometime between the age of thirty-two and thirty-four, a batsman, however great, loses his bearings. We call this phenomenon 'the thirty-three effect'.

This period usually witnesses a sharp decline in batting power. Some recover, others never do. What is interesting about this phase is that it's usually preceded by one of immense dominance where the player is usually compared with the best ever. Also, this is the phase where sponsors usually invest significantly in a player thinking that the form he displayed over the last couple of years will persist over the next two to three years as well.

But nothing of the sort happens. On the contrary, the batsman—irrespective of whether he is a composed technically correct batsman or a 'natural' uninhibited stroke-player—often loses the plot. Why does this happen? We do not know why this happens. Perhaps it is some physiological process, either kicking in or failing to. Or perhaps it is the brain sending a signal to the body that it's time to think of a different career. We are not neurologists but can share some perspectives from people more knowledgeable in this field.

The recent works of some well-known neurologists have done much to increase general understanding of how the brain works. In *Phantoms in the Brain*, V.S. Ramachandran and Sandra Blakeslee describe an interesting phenomenon in the chapter 'The Zombie in the Brain', which is relevant to athletic and sporting performance. They talk of an experiment conducted by Dr Salvatore Aglioti where two identical circles were placed, one surrounded by smaller secondary circles and the other by larger secondary ones. This created the visual impression of one of the two identical circles—the one surrounded by smaller secondary circles—looking larger. But when these circles were replaced by dominos of the same size (in a game of dominos) and the same observer was asked to pick it up, the hand stretched to the same extent for both the central circles, meaning that the brain sends the right signal to the hands. In other words, while the eye is fooled by the picture below, the brain is not.

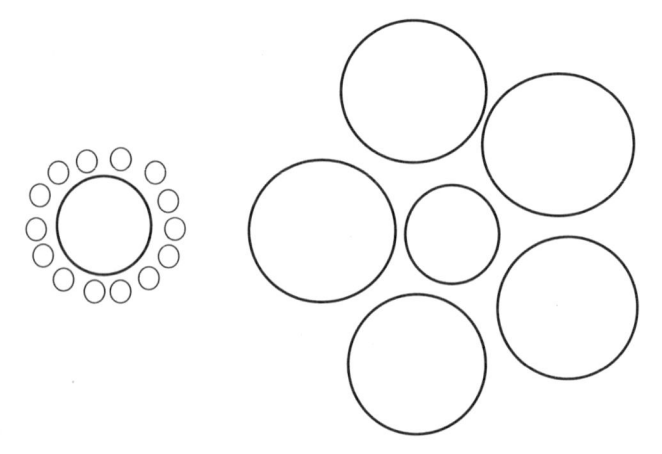

Figure 1: These are two central circles surrounded by secondary circles. To the left the secondary circles are smaller, to the right, larger. The eye sees the central circle on the left as larger than the central circle on the right, but the brain isn't fooled!

The signal from the brain to the body is not consistent with the signal from the eye to the brain. This ability to decide on 'how' to act differing from 'what' you see has been defined as the zombie in the brain, which is able to decode reality from misleading perception. This has immense significance for sportsmen. Dr Ramachandran goes on to explain how marksmen say that they need to 'let go' to hit the bull's eye and not focus too much. Quarterbacks throw the ball not where outfielders currently stand, but where they would if there was no interception. Outfielders, much before they see the ball, start calculating its position as soon as they hear the crack of ball on bat; what happens here is that a pathway in the parietal lobe converts auditory input into the expected destination of ball as an output. Ramachandran's observation is that in sports and in other aspects of life, releasing this inexplicable zombie mechanism is crucial to success. So perhaps it is not the 'eye' that goes when players lose their reflexes, but this zombie mechanism, which is able to decode where the ball should be.

The good news is that the brain is able to readjust, but there is a painful period where the signal mechanism appears to be less than 100 per cent, and this, we speculate, seems to kick in about the age of thirty-three in a cricketing context for batsmen.

Table I (on page 44) outlines the Test averages of some great batsmen of the last four decades, with a focus on how they did in their early thirties. It shows that somewhere between the age of thirty-two and thirty-four, their average drops by 10–20 runs—a significant fall. They usually hike it back for one to three years before a more permanent decline sets in.

Table I: The Thirty-three Effect

Player	Career average	The 'Thirty-three Effect' around	Test averages by season
Gordon Greenidge (b. 1 May 1951)	44.72	1984	1982–83: 78.60 1984: 81.74 1984–85: 36.76 1985–86: 36.16 1986–87: 47.60
Garfield Sobers (b. 28 July 1936)	57.78	1969	1966–67: 114.00 1967–68: 90.83 1968–69: 37.80 1969: 30.00 1970–71: 74.62
Adam Gilchrist (b. 14 November 1971)	48.66	2004	2002–03: 56.69 2003 (1 innings): 43.00 2003–04: 35.83 2004: 28.75 2004–05: 69.07
Matthew Hayden (b. 29 October 1971)	53.00	2004	2003–04: 82.33 2004: 72.00 2004–05: 33.10 2005: 35.33 2005–06: 58.50
Vivian Richards (b. 7 March 1952)	50.23	1985	1985–86: 66.20 1986–87: 28.00 1987–88: 63.66

Sunil Gavaskar	51.12	1982	1981–82: 62.50
(b. 10 July 1949)			1982: 24.66
			1982–83: 46.27
Geoff Boycott	47.72	1975	1973: 58.00
(b. 21 October 1942)			1973–74: 46.77
			1974: 8.00
			(1 Test)
			Did not play till 1977
			1977: 147.33
Rahul Dravid	52.61	2006	2005–06: 43.41
(b. 11 January 1973)			2006: 43.43
			2006–07: 20.83
			2007: 39.75
			despite help from
			Bangladesh Tests
			2007-08: 37.87
Javed Miandad	52.57	1989	1988–89: 114.42
(b. 12 June 1957)			1989–90: 46.90
			1990–91: 24.71
			1991–92: 12.33
			1992: 60.66
Greg Chappell	53.86	1981	1979–80: 64.53
(b. 7 August 1948)			1980: 53.00
			1981: 40.85
			1982–3: 50.55

What happened to the above greats also happened to Tendulkar. The figures for him are as follows:

Table II: The Thirty-three Effect for Sachin Tendulkar

	Career average	The 'Thirty-three Effect' starts around	Test averages by season
Sachin Tendulkar (b. 24 April 1973)	55.31	2006	2003–04: 54.91
			2004–05: 55.33
			2005–06: 27.91
			2006–07: 33.16
			2007: 60.25
			2007–08: 63.20

Tendulkar would have had reasons to be confident in 2003, having topped the World Cup run charts in South Africa, and played one defining innings in a knock-out match against Pakistan. But as he entered 2004, there were warning signs. In the two-Test series against South Africa, he was relatively quiet. He averaged 27.5 at a modest strike rate of 40.44. But a supporting 32 not out in the second Test in Calcutta, which helped India to a win, ensured that alarm bells weren't going off—not yet.

The next series against Bangladesh was productive—as any series against Bangladesh tends to be—and he averaged 284, with an unbeaten 248 being the main contribution. A day might come when Bangladesh, like Sri Lanka, will shake the cricketing world as they have shown a positive intent, at least in ODIs. But as of now, in Tests, averages against Bangladesh do not signify anything special in terms of performance. The series against Pakistan in March 2005 saw Sachin averaging a respectable 51.00 at a strike rate of 45.21. But his overall performance was disappointing, primarily for one reason: the Bangalore

Test. Chasing 383 to win on the final day of the final Test, India could not bat out the day. Despite the fact that several teams fail to bat out the fifth day nowadays, what was troubling was the manner of Tendulkar's (16 off 98 balls) and Dravid's (16 off 64 balls) batting, which pointed to a negativity in approach. In the case of Tendulkar, given his preference for dominating the bowling, this was even more distressing. As a consequence of the defensive strategy, the Pakistani spin bowlers could set a close field and bowl out India. Afridi had figures of 17-7-13-3 and Arshad Khan 14-8-21-2—and neither is quite renowned to set the stands on fire as a bowler. To those watching the proceedings, Tendulkar's negativism set off alarm bells, raising doubts on his fitness, mindset and positive intent.

Sri Lanka came to India in December 2005 and the lassitude continued, with Sachin aggregating 189 runs in three Tests at an average of 37.8 and a strike rate of 42.4. Tendulkar's main achievement in this series was a landmark 109 in the second Test at Delhi, with which he topped the list of century makers in the history of Test cricket. This milestone was significant enough to assuage any concerns about the strike rate in the Sri Lanka series.

The Times of India *Declares 'Endulkar?':* *Or Why We Shouldn't Believe Everything We Read*

The next series in Pakistan started in January 2006, three months before Tendulkar's thirty-third birthday. In this series, the wheels officially came off the cart. He got 63 runs at an average of 21 with a highest score of 26. This is when the muted criticism turned into a crescendo with several insinuations that Tendulkar was past it, especially with regard to short-pitched fast bowling. The England series at home that followed was no better, with Sachin aggregating just 83 runs in three Tests at an average of 20.75. In the Bombay Test, India, chasing 313, were bowled out for 100. Tendulkar got 34 of those, but Shaun Udal got 4 for 14 from 9.3 overs, bowling India out to level the series 1-1. For Shaun Udal, aged thirty-seven, and with a bowling average of 92 coming into the Test, it was a match to remember. But what happened on the second day of the Test was hitherto unthinkable. A part of the crowd booed Tendulkar after he was dismissed for 1 (off 21 balls) in the first innings. For Tendulkar, it was a reminder of the fickleness of the mob. An English journalist referred to Tendulkar as a 'walking wicket'.

Could things get any worse? There was a brief respite for Sachin in South Africa in December 2006 with a combative 44 (walking in at 14 for 2) on a green top against an excellent South African bowling attack of Dale Steyn, Makhaya Ntini, Graeme Pollock, Jacques Kallis and Andre Nel. India won the first Test, but proceeded to lose the next. In the third Test in Cape Town, Sachin's second innings batting attitude brought back memories of Bangalore's fifth-day deer-in-the-headlights performance against Pakistan earlier. Having got a 41-run lead in the first innings with South Africa to bat last, the Indian cricket fan could be forgiven for expecting success or at worst a draw. But with a scratchy 14 off 62 balls, Tendulkar revived all the old fears. The Indian fans expected him to take on Paul Harris, the debutant spinner, but in tandem with Rahul Dravid he put on 24 runs in 15.1 excruciating overs. South Africa hit up the 211 needed without too much drama, and a series, which had started promisingly, ended in disappointment.

In an article entitled 'Watching Sachin Was Embarrassing', Sambit Bal wrote in Cricinfo on 5 January 2007: 'Tendulkar pottered and scratched, padded and swivelled, nudged and groped and the Indian innings came to a standstill. ... from Tendulkar, there was simply no intent.'

There are times when criticism has to be accepted, howsoever painful. We disagree with Sambit on some other issues, but on this particular Tendulkar innings, he was spot on. Not surprisingly then, after several series where his batting had been uncharacteristically subdued, the question for fan and fanatic alike was: is this going to be the Sachin we see henceforth? More disturbingly, what if it gets worse?

The following away series against Bangladesh saw Tendulkar average 127 and aggregate 254 in two Tests. But the real test lay ahead. Coming up were two ordeals by fire—tours to England and Australia. By the time the England series started, Tendulkar would be over thirty-four. So the questions in our mind were: had the body learnt to adjust to the ageing process and would we see the Tendulkar of old again?

There is a proverb in Tamil that says 'a king even in a mud house is majestic and a conch shell shines even when burnt'. The 2006 series in Pakistan, where the wheels came off the cart, saw some sparkling batting in the ODIs, with 234 runs from four matches at an average of 59.25. Of particular interest was a skilful 95 off 104 balls, which enabled India to chase down 288 after they were 14 for 2 at one time on a wicket that had plenty for Mohammad Asif and Umar Gul. In the same year, there was also a sparkling 141 not out versus the West Indies in Kuala Lumpur in a triangular tournament also involving Australia. Later on 31 January 2007, there was a memorable

100 off 76 balls in the series decider against the West Indies in a home series, which made him the man of the match and the man of the series.

But these were reminders of the past rather than assurances for the future. *The Times of India* on 1 February 2006, carried a provocative feature by Siddhartha Mishra entitled 'Endulkar', virtually announcing the end of an era. To quote from it:

> It may seem churlish to question his credentials after one bad series, but ask yourself one question—when was the last time Sachin inspired confidence while facing up to genuinely high-quality opposition on a juicy wicket? ... If hell-raisers point out that Shoaib Akhtar's speed succeeded in reducing Sachin to a dartboard in pads, it is not without basis.

The article went on to quote such 'experts' on the art of batsmanship as Maninder Singh, Kirti Azad, W.V. Raman and Surinder Khanna on what Tendulkar should do next. Another worthy, Moin Khan, declared in a separate article that in the second Test in Faisalabad in January 2006, Tendulkar had walked when he was not out as he was disinclined to face Shoaib Akhtar.

In short, this was a phase where everyone had a lot of advice for Tendulkar. If Tendulkar himself was worried, he didn't talk about it publicly.

Ian Chappell's Mirror

The World Cup 2007 in the West Indies was for many reasons an unfortunate event. Although Adam Gilchrist redeemed a shambolic final, circumstances around Bob Woolmer's death overshadowed the event. Some things are much more important than cricket.

The World Cup was a disaster for the Indian team and Tendulkar. For the team, there was an ongoing war between Greg Chappell and Ganguly, which has been well documented. Further news of rifts and lobbies seeped through to the press. Assuming there is no smoke without fire, one can at the very least conclude that communication within the team and between players was very poor, if not absent. If Tendulkar's World Cup in 2003 had been a success, the 2007 edition was a personal nadir in terms of ODI form. An average of 32.00 in three games conceals failures in two games which India had to win to qualify for the next stage—the ones against Bangladesh and Sri Lanka where his personal contributions were 7 and 0, respectively.

Ian Chappell wrote a much-discussed article in Cricinfo at that time (30 March 2007). The article, which we call 'Mirror, Mirror', made four points. One, that Sachin was playing to accumulate statistics and not to win matches for the team. Two, that Lara had not changed his style or effectiveness while Sachin had diminished from being a class player to an average one. Three, that even his 241 not out at Sydney was a 'classic case of a great player really struggling'. Finally, that he was wasting his time if he was trying to accumulate statistics and should retire immediately.

The article ended with the following words: 'If Tendulkar had found an honest mirror three years ago and asked the question: "Mirror, mirror on the wall, who is the best batsman of all?" it would have answered: "Brian Charles Lara." If he asked that same mirror right now: "Mirror, mirror on the wall, should I retire?" The answer would be: "Yes."'

We have no qualms about people articulating negative facts or opinions on Sachin—that is the prerogative of commentators and writers. That Sachin had a poor run with his bat during the 'fall' phase is a fact. We also understand and, as unbiased cricket fans, agree with opinions like Sambit Bal's on the Cape Town second innings and have to swallow the bitter pill of truth. We also think that debates are normal; for example, the debate on his 241 not out at Sydney 2004 has ranged from Ian Chappell's negative assessment on the one hand to Shane Warne's positive evaluation, using this innings to argue why he rates Sachin higher than Lara, on the other, and Harsha Bhogle's view that it was one of the top innings he had seen as a commentator. To put it on record, we view this as one of the greatest innings Sachin has played in his career—bringing to play his totally focused mind and his enormous will power. More importantly, from the point of view of the team (which Ian Chappell has been harping on!), he had set up the match and given a great chance for India to win a Test series in Australia. Unfortunately (but not surprisingly), our bowlers ('assisted' by Parthiv Patel's bloopers as wicketkeeper) lost the rare opportunity—they could neither get Jason Gillespie (a tail-ender) in the first innings early nor get Australia out in the second innings despite having more than a day to do so. Where Ian Chappell has erred is in attributing non-existent motives to Sachin's style in the past and speculating recklessly about the future. Sachin has proven his motives to play for India over many years and he would do so again in the year just after the article was published.

With any other player having a bad patch we would focus primarily on the player. But with Sachin, we need to go beyond the player. For Sachin is not just a player; he is much more—a whole ecosystem!

The Tendulkar Ecosystem

Tendulkar is a cricketer, but he is also an industry, almost an ecosystem. There are several people feeding off the Tendulkar effect. Firstly, the media companies who thrive on the incremental effect on TRPs when Tendulkar is playing. Then there are the state associations whose media incomes and gate receipts are boosted by the Tendulkar draw card. For confirmation, you only have to ask the Nagpur Cricket Association that saw its gate sales triple when Tendulkar was declared fit for the Test versus Australia on 26 October 2004. Then there are the sponsors who make millions selling products endorsed by him. Finally, there is the collective self-image of the Indian cricket fan and fanatic, not to forget Team India!

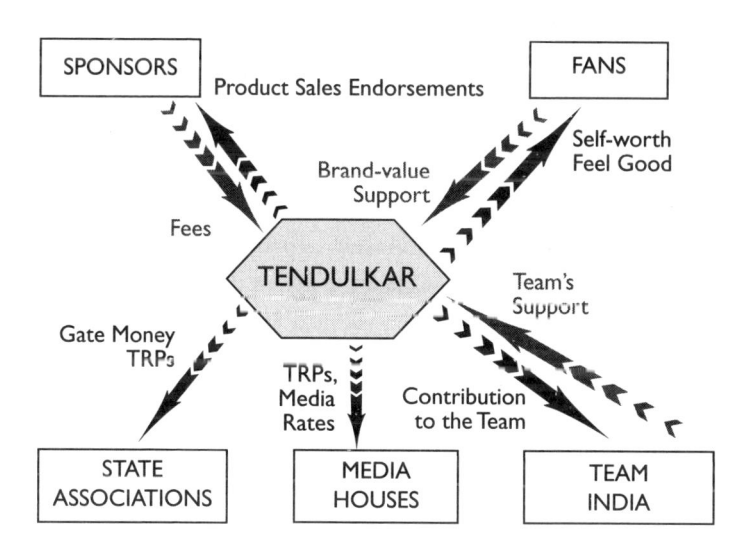

What all this does is perhaps make Tendulkar play when he shouldn't. We believe Sachin should not have played in the Nagpur and Bombay Tests against Australia in 2004. Why did he? Only Sachin can answer that but we share what we think happened. India versus Australia has been the most important Test series in cricket over the last decade or so. India has never won a series in Australia and Australia had not won a series in India for over thirty years. Steve Waugh had called winning in India the 'last frontier' in the modern era in the game. Sachin has always contributed well in Test matches against Australia and he has always wanted to play against the best. He was desperate to play from the first Test but his elbow had not healed enough. Without Sachin, India lost in Bangalore in the first Test and missed the opportunity to win in Madras in the second Test partly due to our bowlers' incapability to get Gillespie out (again!) and partly because the last day's play was washed out by rain.

Sachin went on to play the third Test despite his elbow not having healed. Why? Firstly, the team needed him to try to prevent the 'last frontier' from falling. Second, the rest of the ecosystem needed him—for example, we have shared the data on the gate collection and the fans' expectations.

When Tendulkar approached the age of thirty-three, he got a quadruple whammy. Firstly, there was the tendonitis. Then there was the thirty-three effect. Add to that the continuous pressure of fans to play despite injury. Finally, he just didn't look happy or engaged in the game. We don't know why. Perhaps it was fatigue, perhaps it was biological change. The same Tendulkar who reacted to spin the way a glutton looks at chocolate mousse, was strangely tied to the crease against the likes of Paul Harris and Shaun Udal.

At this stage, Tendulkar had, as per our understanding from the media, two rounds of elbow problems and one shoulder injury. His movements appeared constrained, and his natural intent to come down the wicket was hampered. Common sense suggested a long gap from the game to rehabilitate himself. But what then of the ecosystem?

To understand deeply the importance of the ecosystem, let us see a national debate arising from the criticism of one of his strident critics, Sanjay Manjrekar, who argued, in an article in *The Times of India* (24 July 2006), that Tendulkar's fear of failing when he is anything less than 100 per cent physically fit kept him away from the game during that period. Manjrekar even questioned the timing and duration of the master batsman's healing process from injuries. While the article stressed that Tendulkar, at this stage of his career when he is no longer a teenager, would do well to make use of all the playing opportunities that come his way, the bigger question posed by the *Times of India* debate was whether Manjrekar's criticism was justified.

We have a personal litmus test on whether Tendulkar is on song or not, which involves observing how he plays the first ball when it is pitched on middle and leg. If it goes racing to the leg-side boundary, then it's business as usual. When it doesn't, our amber flag goes up. And when he plays spin with respect, the flag turns to red.

We do not know what it is to be a star player. But what we do suspect is that, after some time, it is not the player who owns the fans, but the fans who own the player who probably feels compelled to show up despite the mind, body and doctors all saying no. This was not the first time Tendulkar had played when others simply wouldn't. The first was just after his father's demise during the World Cup in England when he had to play to meet the expectations of the team and his fans.

How tiresome it must be to be deified. Particularly by those blessed with a short memory and a sense of ingratitude. How tiresome it must be to answer irrational prayers day in and day out. How tiresome it must be to carry the hopes of millions, who will turn against you the moment you fail.

Tendulkar was jeered in Bombay when India lost to England. To the non-Indian, this is equivalent to Maradona being heckled in Argentina. It is simply inconceivable—something beyond the realm of possibilities. In Bombay, it came to pass. We were reminded of the instances when Indian fanatics turned against some great cricketers. Sunil Gavaskar got stoned in Calcutta. Bishen Bedi got the full treatment after India lost to Pakistan in 1977. When Tendulkar got the 'treatment' in Bombay, he responded differently to what Gavaskar did. Gavaskar had decided to never again play in Calcutta; then he tempered down his criticism, reconciled with the Bengali fans, and eventually, his son, Rohan, ended up playing for the Bengal team. But Tendulkar responded with silence and runs. He clearly feels a deep sense of responsibility to the cricket fanatics in India no matter how undeserving.

This is the price of being deified. To have to continuously be accountable to the undeserving.

The Hidden Face of God

In the Old Testament, the behavioural pattern of God is fascinating. Initially, He is concerned with breathing life into man, fashioning woman out of man's ribs and getting deeply involved in the daily affairs of humanity. As time passes, and as the ungratefulness of the human race increases, He distances himself from man, His involvement becomes less intense. Finally, He tells Moses: 'I shall hide my face from them/I shall see what their end will be' (Deut. 31:17, 18; 32:20).

And that is the last we hear from God directly in the Bible. Not one word thereafter. This is beautifully described by Richard E. Friedman in his book, *The Hidden Face of God*. (Not to be confused with a book by Gerald L. Schroeder with the same name.) The point we wish to make is that whether we fashion a God or vice versa, the trend of ingratitude of man (or fan), followed by indifference of God (real or in cricketing terms), is not hard to understand.

Tendulkar would have been justified in packing his bags after being jeered in his home town. He would have been justified in walking away from the fans, fanatics, sponsors, team-mates, media companies and other beneficiaries in the Tendulkar ecosystem. But he didn't, and went on to script another story altogether.

6
The Resurrection

Surely this was a moment decreed by the gods.

—MIKE COWARD, *The Australian*, on Sachin's century at Adelaide, 24 January 2008

In a seminal article titled 'Accepting the Master's Change', on 16 December 2004, Sambit Bal made a pertinent point. He mentioned that Tendulkar had played more than fifteen years of international cricket, more than Allan Border's entire playing span. Sunil Gavaskar played for sixteen and Viv Richards for seventeen. Tendulkar's exploits have spanned thirteen countries and ninety-five grounds and he has scored more runs and more hundreds than anyone else in the history of the game. Yet, as Bal notes, we refuse to accept that Tendulkar has aged, matured, slowed down. 'We continue to expect the fizz and abandon of a 19-year-old from a 31-year-old man ... We refuse to acknowledge that the body can slow down, the mind can become weary and mindful of pitfalls. Quite simply, we just can't bear the thought of our Sachin growing old.'

Bal closed his article by quoting Peter Roebuck: 'No regrets should be held about Tendulkar acknowledging the passing of time and becoming a robust, rather than a dazzling batsman. He must be allowed to grow. Watching him bat may not be as exciting, but it will be enormously satisfying. Those who love their cricket will be given the opportunity of watching a master at work.'

For some reason, many people view changing the game as a sign of weakness. Perhaps, as Bal argues, these people just can't bear the thought of a great sportsman growing old. The fact is that some of the greatest champions (for example,

Muhammad Ali and Tiger Woods) have changed their strategies to win. Adaptability is a sign of strength rather than a weakness. In fact, not changing might make a champion look ordinary. Bal gives a strong example of the perils of not adapting: Viv Richards's last years as a cricketer, when despite slowing reflexes he never let go of the anger and the swagger. So that he either blazed away or perished. It is telling that in the last three years Richards managed only 978 runs from 19 Tests at 36.22 with only one century. Bal concludes, 'Richards was too proud a man to defend, but he was a lesser player for it during his last years.'

At the time Bal's article was published, the decline of Sachin was not evident; in fact, it could have been argued that he had changed his game and had successfully adapted. The real evidence of the fall came later—as discussed in the previous chapter. After the World Cup of 2007, many Sachin fans secretly despaired that the end was near and that it would be a tame end. Some critics (like Ian Chappell) wrote Sachin's cricketing epitaph. For fans, the million-dollar question was: 'How will his career end?'

So, what was the 2007–08 season going to bring for Sachin (and his innumerable fans)? Would Sachin disappear from the firmament, struggle like a journeyman, or resurrect himself with a changed game? How about a resurrection via a rediscovery of the Sachin of 1998 vintage! What were the odds of that happening? Let us summarize Sachin's record between 24 March 2007—when India was knocked out of the World Cup—and 23 March 2008:

Table I: Sachin, March 2007–March 2008

Format	Number of Matches	Runs	Period Average/ Career Average	Period Strike Rate/ Career Strike Rate	Centuries	90s	Other Fifties
Tests	11	1114	65/55	57/54	4	1	5
ODI	33	1514	47/44	83/85	1	7	5

This is the record of a batsman who, according to Chappell's mirror, ought to have retired!

Let us understand this better: in Tests, Sachin scored a fifty in every match except at Lord's, and registered a score above ninety in almost 25 per cent of the ODIs. This is the kind of consistency that typifies a great batsman. This is the 'what' part of the answer, but we will delve deeper series by series on 'how' Sachin made these 2628 runs in one year and in what context: did he gather it by pottering around against weaklings or did he blaze, 1998 style, against the strongest opponents? A thought: If he had not been afflicted by the jinx of the nineties, he would have made thirteen international centuries in one year! Was he polishing his stats or winning for India?

Sachin's year started with a Test series in Bangladesh. Two Tests, two centuries. We won't comment. But if he had failed, his critics would have rubbed their hands with glee, written much and invited readers to comment on blogs on why he ought to retire.

Next up was the ODI series against South Africa in Ireland. India had not won an away series ever against South Africa, and of all opponents, Sachin's record against the Proteas was relatively weak. India went on to win the series and Sachin became the man of the series with two nineties. The second one, 93 off 106 balls, was a real gem; more importantly, he was hooking and pulling against Ntini and Nel. Were we seeing the Sachin of old? The innings would indicate just that.

The first Test against England at Lord's was Sachin's solitary failure in a year when he played eleven Tests. It is interesting that this one failure was enough for the critics to draw out the knives. This is why we say: a short memory and ingratitude are the defining characteristics of the Indian cricket fan/fanatic. It must be infinitely galling for Sachin to be judged on his last innings after having played nearly two decades.

India barely survived the Lord's Test. In the second Test in Nottingham, Sachin top scored with 91. His unbroken partnership with Ganguly in the pre-lunch session of the third day against good bowling (especially Ryan Sidebottom in seaming conditions) was what opened the game up for India, an opportunity that Zaheer Khan then grabbed with both hands. This innings played a crucial role in setting up victory in the match and ultimately the series. In that innings, Sachin seemed destined to get a biggie, but alas, the best umpire in the world, Simon Taufel, made a rare blunder. He did apologize the next day, but the scorebook will forever show 91. Sachin made 82 in the last Test at the Oval, but the Test will perhaps be remembered primarily for the debate on whether Dravid made the correct decision in not asking England to follow-on.

In the ODI series against England, Sachin made 99 in Bristol, a venue he seems to be fond of. But then India went down 1-3 with three games to go. Once again, it was up to Sachin to help India to get on its feet: 71 runs off only 59 balls in Leeds and 94 runs off only 81 balls at the Oval as India levelled the series at 3-3. But the finale at Lord's was marred by poor umpiring, with both Dravid and Sachin being the victims. And it was Aleem Dar's turn to apologize a couple of months later!

Sachin's performance was not exactly brilliant in the ODI series against Australia in late 2007 at home. Yet, he top scored in Chandigarh with 79 as India won, made a 'lone-ranger' 47 in Baroda, a 72 off 72 balls in Nagpur, a match which India ought to have won but lost, and a winning 21 in a low-scoring match in Bombay.

Soon after, in the ODIs against Pakistan at home, Sachin was in dazzling form. His 99 in Mohali and 97 in Gwalior were of the highest quality; in fact, the 97 in Gwalior got India the series and confirmed that the Sachin of '98 was back.

In the first Test against Pakistan in November–December 2007, Sachin closed an unfinished chapter. In 1999, despite his second innings score of 136, India had lost narrowly. India has had a poor record of finishing off Test matches. But in Delhi, Sachin was there till the end with 56 not out as India won the Test and, with draws in the next two Tests, this helped India to win the series eventually. After an 82 in Calcutta, he got injured and didn't play in the last, drawn Test.

If the resurrection of Sachin Tendulkar in 2007–08 was poetic, then the climax to the year was even more so. It evokes one of the famous poems of Alfred Tennyson, 'Ulysses'. Ulysses was a legendary king of an island called Ithaca, and was fond of great voyages. Tennyson writes: 'To follow knowledge like a sinking star,/Beyond the utmost bound of human thought.' That is almost akin to Sachin who has always set high standards for himself, forever in the pursuit of new benchmarks.

Sachin was once interviewed during the time he was recovering from his elbow surgery. The interviewer asked him about the elusive thirty-fifth Test century and other such record-related matters, and Sachin replied, 'You don't understand—you keep asking questions about records. The most important thing for me is to be able to play for India. It is difficult to describe to you what it feels like not to be able to even lift the bat!' Again, Tennyson's lines sum up this agony: 'How dull it is to pause, to make an end/ To rust unburnish'd, not to shine in use!'

Let us now focus on the Tests and ODI series in Australia, the toughest away tour for any country. Once Dravid resigned as the captain, many, including the selectors, wanted Sachin to lead the Test team in the series against Pakistan at home and against Australia away. But Sachin turned this down, much like Ulysses, who gave up his throne and asked his son to be the king. Being the captain was not the important motivation; what mattered was the trip to Australia, perhaps his last tour there. Sachin's feelings perhaps echo Ulysses', as the Ithacan warms up to the prospect of voyage and says with much eagerness: 'There lies the port; the vessel puffs her sail.'

Sachin knew that most of the 'seniors' on the tour would not travel to Australia for a series again; he also knew that in the past, he had to play like a lonely warrior and suffered much (like in 1999). Critics thought that Sachin would fail against fearsome bowlers like Brett Lee on lively Australian pitches. But Ulysses thought differently: 'Old age hath yet his honour and his toil;/ Some work of noble note, may yet be done.'

We start with the bare statistics of the tour of Australia, without providing any context: in four Tests (eight innings), Sachin made 493 runs at an average of 70.42 (as against his career average of 55.31) and at a strike rate of 65.64 (as against his career strike rate of 54.05) with two centuries (Sydney and Adelaide) and two fifties (Melbourne and Perth)—i.e., he scored well in each of the four Tests. In ten ODIs, Sachin made 399 runs at an average of 44.33 (as against his career average of 44.33—yes, remarkable!) and at a strike rate of 85.25 (compared to his career strike rate of 85.49).

These bare stats prove that there was 'some work of noble note' done indeed! With context, one can appreciate the real value of the work.

In the Boxing Day Test in Melbourne 2007, Kumble led the charge to restrict Australia to 343. India's batting woes started even before the toss. The captain and the selectors made a couple of connected blunders. In their anxiety to push Yuvraj Singh into the team, Virender Sehwag (yes, the hero of the Boxing Day Test in 2003) was dropped and Dravid was asked to open. In the first session of the second day, India lost the initiative that the bowlers had grabbed. Sachin walked in to play just after lunch, when India was 31 for 2, made at a crawling pace off 21.4 overs. Jaffer made 4 off 27 balls and Dravid 5 off 66 balls. For the nth time, India was very dependent on Sachin Tendulkar. Sachin changed the tempo dramatically, scoring 62 off 77 balls. When his partnership with Ganguly (43) was on, it seemed that India was back in the game; but as so often before, once Sachin fell, the team crashed. The bad old days of the 1990s (when Sachin had waged a lone battle in the same ground in 1999) had returned.

The Sydney Test is worthy of a novel—of heroism, character, the turns and twists of vintage Test cricket on the one hand, and appalling umpiring and plain cheating by the Australians on the other. But all that will be for a different day, a different book. For now, we will only cherish Sachin's majestic 154 not out and the standing ovation the Sydney crowd gave him. Mike Coward's piece titled 'Appreciative Crowd Affords Giant of

Game Bradmanesque Reception' (*The Australian*, 5 January 2008) said all that had to be said. He wrote:

> This was a moment to treasure always. 'I was there' will become a lifetime refrain of those privileged to be at the historic SCG yesterday.
>
> For 127 years the game's greatest players have celebrated their art at this special place and earned the plaudits of the grateful citizens of the city.
>
> But aside Don Bradman, surely few can have received such a sustained and emotional ovation as that accorded the diminutive giant of the contemporary game, Sachin Tendulkar.
>
> When the little maestro completed his second run through cover point to complete his 38th hundred and eighth against Australia, the crowd of 29,358 rose as one to acknowledge not just this innings but his undisputed greatness as a batsman.

All we want to add to that is that one of us (Vijay) was there at the venue on that day with his mother and a dear friend—'I was there' indeed with 29,355 other people.

For the record, India lost the Test, thus conceding a 0-2 deficit with the real threat of an ignominious 0-4 drubbing looming large. This alone made the context of the Perth Test very tough; add to that the psychological scar in Sydney, and Australia's record at Perth, which is called 'Australia's Bank', where no subcontinental team had won ever. And then the media went to town about the fearsome pitch and Shaun Tait's pace in tandem with Brett Lee. When Sachin arrived at 59 for 2, the question was: could he roll back the years and play something on the lines of his memorable 114 in Perth, which he made as a teenager? One hundred and thirty-nine runs later, with Sachin's audacious 71, the answer was obvious. Not only could he still play the upper cut as well as he did sixteen years earlier, he also improvised an out-of-the-world boundary against Lee whose express delivery was headed towards Sachin's head. An average batsman could have been injured seriously. A good batsman could have avoided the ball awkwardly. A great batsman could have ducked with elegance. Sachin saw the ball, arched his body superbly and played the ball high above the keeper's head and scored a boundary! A sequence of photos showed how Sachin's eyes never left the ball till it was cut away: a master class on keeping the eyes on the ball all the time.

There is karma in life—India won much more than a Test.

In possibly his last Test match in Australia, Sachin made a century. This 153 in Adelaide, Bradman's home, was most apt. The knock, a culmination of his batting in Australian soil, prompted Nagraj Gallopade of Cricinfo to call Sachin an 'Australian idol'.

With hardly any break, the show moved to the CB triangular series between India, Australia and Sri Lanka. In the first seven matches, Sachin didn't play well even though he top scored in one of them which India won against Australia. Even after over 25,000 international runs, even after a fantastic resurrection, post-March 2007, even after 493 runs against Australia in the just concluded Test series, there were critics like S. Rajesh of Cricinfo (stat editor) and Sanjay Manjrekar who were laying it on thick. Rajesh dwelt on Sachin's record in contributing to India's run chases in ODIs 'recently', and Manjrekar (25 February 2008 in *The Times of India*) said, 'But with Tendulkar, it's like the elephant in the room that no one wants to talk about.'

Sachin silenced his critics in the virtual semifinal against Lanka with a winning 63 while chasing, something the critics said he was not doing well. He followed it up with a glorious 117 not out in the first final in Sydney that India won, again chasing, securing him the man of the match award. He top-scored with 91 in the second final; most importantly, he helped India win the second final too, thus winning the series. Most cricket followers would rate the CB series win as the most important accomplishment in Indian cricket's ODI history, after the triumphs at the 1983 World Cup and the 1985 Benson and Hedges.

To capture the year of Sachin's resurrection in all its poetic beauty, it's again time to turn to 'Ulysses', this time its last stanza:

> We are not now that strength which in old days
> Moved earth and heaven; that which we are, we are;
> One equal temper of heroic hearts,
> Made weak by time and fate, but strong in will
> To strive, to seek, to find, and not to yield.

7
The Case against Sachin Tendulkar

If he asked that same mirror right now, 'Mirror, mirror on the wall, should I retire?' the answer would be, 'Yes.'

—IAN CHAPPELL, March 2007

One would have thought that after nearly twenty years of top notch performances there wouldn't be any aspect of Tendulkar's game one could carp about, that a man who has scored over 28,000 international runs, including over eighty international centuries, will not need any justification. But as anyone following Indian cricket knows, Indian cricketers are scrutinized more than most. And Sachin, for all his heroics, has had his share of strident criticism with critics harping on some aspects of his record to make their case against him. There is no harm in this; we defend the right of the critic to criticize. But as some players, like Sachin, don't write books in their own defence we will address the critics' charges. We will look at each of these points of criticism to provide our rejoinder and lay to rest the case against Sachin once and for all. The case against Tendulkar consists of some aspects of his record, each of which will be analysed in detail.

Tendulkar Is Not a Match Winner

During the 1990s, when Tendulkar was at his peak, the Indian team did not win many matches, or at the very least as many matches as they should have if they had 'God' in their midst.

The origins of the charge lie in the opinions expressed by some iconic ex-cricketers. Let us revisit some of these opinions. Former Pakistan captain and speedster Imran Khan, on

7 October 2002, said that Tendulkar was not a match winner when compared to Viv Richards, and that he still needed to perform at crucial times (http://www.indiaabroad.com/cricket/2003/oct/06ten.htm). 'He must perform at crucial times when you need him to perform. My point is that when you compare Sachin Tendulkar to Viv Richards, he is not a match winner. The greatness of a player is also to perform at the right time.'

On 25 July 2007, former Indian captain and all-rounder Kapil Dev told Aaj Tak, a Hindi news channel: 'Every time people hope big things from Sachin Tendulkar, but often it is only disappointment that we are left with. He is thought to be the backbone of the Indian team but many times he has not stood up to the occasion.' Kapil's outburst came in the wake of Tendulkar's failure to play a match-winning knock against England in the second innings at Lord's in 2007 with India set to chase 380. Tendulkar fell to Monty Panesar for 16 on the fourth evening, ruled out leg before in front of off-stump. He believed that Tendulkar had failed to grab the best opportunity he could have hoped for to silence his critics. He was emphatic that figures proved Sachin's inability to perform under pressure and though he had big records to his name, people would raise fingers at him until he won matches for India in difficult and testing conditions. See Table I on page 71 for the overall picture.

Sachin's Record in Big Finals Is Suspect

There have been several ODI tournaments in the Tendulkar era where India reached the final. Yet the team lost a majority of these. The argument goes: surely an all-time great like

Viv Richards, with his love for the big occasion, would have pulled off victories in some of these matches? See Table II for a comparison.

Table I: Team India, Performance 1980–2008

	1 January 1980–31 December 1989	*1 January 1990–31 December 1999*	*1 Jan 2000–9 May 2008*
Tests			
Win	11	18	33
Draw	48 (plus 1 tie)	31	30
Loss	21	20	25
Total Played	81	69	88
Win/loss ratio	0.52	0.90	1.32
ODI			
Win	69	122	130
Loss	80	120	115
Tie		3	
No result	6	12	12
Total Played	155	257	257
Win/loss ratio	0.86	1.01	1.13

Table II: Sachin Tendulkar vs Viv Richards, performance in finals of ODIs

	India in finals with Sachin Tendulkar	*West Indies in finals with Viv Richards*
Played to completion	34	18
Won	15	12
Win percentage	44	66

The questions, by implication, are: Does Tendulkar truly love the big occasion the way Richards did? Or does he put himself under too much pressure and throw his wicket away early (like in the World Cup final against Australia in 2003) in an attempt to score too quickly?

The other, more disturbing, statistic relates to the period between 4 April 1999 and 6 September 2005 when India played twenty-one ODI finals. Surely with 'God' in its midst, the team should have won more than one out of the twenty-one finals it played. Is the Indian team a choker in big finals? And shouldn't Tendulkar, being part of this team, also share the tag?

Tendulkar Plays for Statistics and Not for the Team

The specific case is articulated best in the words of Ian Chappell who commented on 30 March 2007 (http://content-ind.cricinfo.com/ci/content/current/story/287961.html) that Sachin looked like a player 'trying to eke out a career; build on a glittering array of statistics'. He went on to suggest that if indeed that is the case and if Sachin does not help India win as many matches as he can, he should contemplate retirement. It has been separately suggested that Tendulkar's high averages are driven by not outs. For this purpose, a comparison is made between Sachin and the other great of his era, Brian Lara. If Sachin had no not outs, his average would have been 49.5, lower than the cut-off mark of 50 for the greats; whereas Lara's average would still be over 50 at 51.52.

Table III: Sachin Tendulkar vs Brian Lara, a comparison

	Tests played	Innings	Not outs	Runs	Averages
Tendulkar	147	238	25	11782	55.31
Lara	131	232	6	11953	52.88

Tendulkar Changed His Natural Game and Became Conservative in His Approach

Critics have harped on Sachin losing his old flamboyance, suggesting that his approach, bent on bettering his personal average, is hurting the team's interests. It would have been better, critics argue, had he retained the style and flamboyance of his early years even if it had cost him a few points in his average. Without denying in any way his culpability in a couple of uncharacteristic demonstrations of painfully and inexplicably slow batting, one needs to understand that we are at best talking of a few innings in a career spanning hundreds. And of course, as always, we have the facts as laid out in Table IV.

Table IV: Sachin Tendulkar, career strike rate vs strike rate 2003–07

Format	Career strike rate	2003	2004	2005	2006	2007
Tests	54.05	39.43	56.10	44.00	53.50	52.32
ODIs	85.49	87.36	80.07	77.29	77.05	85.58

Tendulkar Has Not Played a Defining Innings That Can Be Placed in the Wisden Top 100

In 2001, *Wisden* compiled its list of the top hundred innings ever played in the history of Test cricket. It covered the period 1876 to 2001. The list contained some beyond-debate great innings like Bradman's 270 versus England at Melbourne in 1936-37 series, Botham's 149 not out at Headingley versus Australia in 1981, Lara's 153 not out versus Australia at Bridgetown in the 1998-89 series and V.V.S. Laxman's epic 281 versus Australia in Calcutta in 2001. However, some interesting inclusions in the list made the exclusion of Sachin Tendulkar quite inexplicable. For example, the list included Ian Redpath's 159 not out where he carried the bat against New Zealand in Auckland in 1974. As New Zealand had been bowled out for 112 in just over 30 overs in their first innings in reply to Australia's first innings score of 221, it was not exactly a close contest that should have merited the inclusion. Another curious choice was Michael Slater's 123 out of Australia's 184 in the second innings at Sydney in 1999. Here, Australia had secured a 102-run first innings lead on a track where Stuart MacGill played havoc with England with match figures of 12 for 107. (Even if Slater had got just 60, Australia would probably have won; such was MacGill's hold on England.)

As such, the following comment from Wisden's Online director, Anthony Bouchier, as reported by *The Times of India* on 28 July 2001, can only be taken with a pinch of salt: 'There is no omission (of Tendulkar) as such. He has not yet scored an innings that merits inclusion in the top 100' (http://timesofindia.indiatimes.com/articleshow/1280158893.cms).

But based on this exclusion, the case against Sachin is: how can a player be called 'God' if he does not have an innings that can find a place in the list of 100 greatest knocks ever?

Tendulkar Has Not Taken India to a 'Famous' Fourth-Innings Victory in a Tense and Exciting Chase

One of the great spectacles in cricket is that of a batsman leading a chase in his team's second innings on the last day of a Test match against a stiff target on a wearing wicket. It is a scenario in which a batsman has to summon nerve and skill and sometimes get the most out of tail-end batsmen. The case against Tendulkar: there are no such scenarios of Tendulkar heroically leading the charge to victory on the last day. The closest he has come is the 136 against Pakistan at Madras in 1999—but here, too, India fell 12 runs short. In fact, his entire fourth-innings average is, well, just average.

Table V: Sachin vs His Peers, Fourth Innings Performance

	Sachin Tendulkar	Brian Lara	Ricky Ponting	Rahul Dravid
Fourth-innings average	33.12	35.12	58.85	46.82
Career average	55.31	52.88	58.53	54.88
Average in fourth innings of matches won	54.83	81.20	92.77	85.40

As far as the victorious Test chases in which Tendulkar has been involved are concerned—four in all—Tendulkar's average, while being a respectable 54.83, is almost thirty to forty less than some of his peers. This is a significant gap in his claim to greatness. So it is evident that Tendulkar has not been able to take his team across the finishing line often enough in Tests, while one of the primary requisites of a great batsman is that he should know how to finish. In Tendulkar's case, there are many instances where he has taken control of the game, but not finished it off.

Tendulkar Has Been Found Wanting Against Strong Opposition in Recent Times

The best players are the ones who perform against the toughest opposition and in adverse conditions. Tendulkar's performance especially between September 2005 and April 2007 has been found wanting against the toughest opposition. This premise was put forward by S. Rajesh of Cricinfo on 7 April 2007 in an article titled 'The Real Culprits' (http://content-www.cricinfo.com/ci/content/story/288746.html). The article spelt out that Indian batsmen had been blaming coach and captain while the real problem was their inability to put up their hands to be counted on in tough conditions. In adverse conditions, the big-name Indian batsmen saw their averages drop alarmingly in ODIs between September 2005 and April 2007: Sachin (55.07 to 27.13), Dravid (60.29 to 29.27), Dhoni (99.4 to 26.41), Ganguly (72.67 to 25.44). On the other hand, Kaif's average in tough conditions went up to 48.78 from a 'good condition' 9.78, while Yuvraj managed a respectable 42.64 in tough conditions, compared to 60.93 when the going was good.

The article then went on to analyse our batsmen's performance against Australia and South Africa in the same period. Sachin's average of 14.09 in eleven innings compared very unfavourably with Yuvraj's 52.25 in five innings or Dravid's 31 in nine innings. For that matter, Kaif had done better with an average of 20.28 in eight innings. Rajesh also pointed out that emotion, hype and selective memory had obscured the facts which the statistical analysis revealed.

Rajesh's article appeared at a time when Indian cricket and its fans were polarized. Either they were with Chappell/Dravid or against them (and pro-Ganguly). Most opinions favoured doing away with the seniors after the debacle of the 2007 World Cup. Here, the statistician was taking a bold stand that the data revealed marquee names failing to perform on the big occasion while a few next-generation players (some cooling their heels on the benches because the seniors weren't making way) and the captain (to some extent) were.

In summary, the case against Tendulkar is that he is not a match winner and has never been a match winner—at his peak, in big finals and in critical situations, as well as in big fourth-innings chases. He can start a chase but cannot finish things off the way a Lara could. And when measured against the very best, and on difficult tracks, he doesn't rate as highly as Ponting, Lara, Dravid and Hayden.

8
The Case for Sachin Tendulkar

Tendulkar handled the pressure when it was most required in the course of a match. He can't do much if your fast bowlers lack firepower ... Tendulkar is still lord of the manor.

—SIR VIVIAN RICHARDS

One of the miracles of modern physics is the 'Observer Paradox' which states that one can never be an observer without being a participant and that there is no reality unless there is an observer.

This is where science and religion begin to meet, because, of course, if there is no one to observe the happenings on this planet, we would not exist. The reason why we make such an observation on observers changing the course of events they watch—at least in their own realities—is brought to life in the following two observations. Both are from great Australians, and both are on Sachin Tendulkar's unbeaten double hundred in Sydney in 2004.

> His double century at the SCG in January 2004 was a classic case of a great player really struggling. He came to the crease out of form and despite amassing all those runs and batting for in excess of ten hours he was no closer to recapturing his best touch than he was when he started out. It was a tribute to his determination but it was a sad sight to see; there are enough average players around that you don't want to see a class one reduced to that level.
>
> —Ian Chappell, as reported in http://content-www.cricinfo.com/ci/content/story/287961.html

I place him very slightly ahead of Lara because I found him slightly tougher mentally. It is such a close call, but here is an example of what I mean: in Australia in 2003-04 he was worried about getting out cover driving so he decided to cut out the shot. I saw the wagon wheel for his next innings: he scored 248 [Sachin scored 241] without a single cover drive.

—Shane Warne, http://www.timesonline.co.uk/tol/ sport/columnists/shane_warne/article2364258.ece

The comments demonstrate one thing: opinions can be divided on the same innings, as seen by two different people. The innings that is used as an example by Chappell on why Sachin should step down, is the very same one that Shane Warne uses to cite why he rates Tendulkar higher than Brian Lara!

We are sure that the criteria Chappell and Warne used for their evaluations, in their minds, are the correct ones. Warne being a great, if not the greatest, spin bowler, appreciates the value of patience and discipline, and Chappell being an unlikely romanticist at heart, possibly appreciates a flashy, attractive fifty or hundred more than a ten-hour epic double hundred. Opinions can be divided on a single innings, and when we talk of Sachin we talk of a career spanning nearly twenty years. So, it isn't a surprise that there is a case against Sachin, and a strong one, highlighted in the previous chapter, and it needs to be argued. That is what we will do here and we will rely heavily on statistics and facts. We will share our views on the facts and data; the conclusions are yours.

When an accusation (or a set of accusations) is made, the defendant's advocates need to do three things to absolve the accused. We will do all three in this chapter: a) defend and explain what really happened, the hard facts, providing the proper context; b) cross-examine the credibility and reliability of witness testimonies; and c) speak forcefully on behalf of the defendant and disprove every charge.

The First Pillar: The Facts

To explain what happened, we must first understand the nature of cricket. Firstly, how many people, even the so-called 'experts', understand, *truly, deeply understand*, that cricket is a multi-player game, a team game, which synergizes the contributions of eleven people?

Secondly to many fans, fanatics and 'pundits', cricket is a batsman's game, which is to say that the team that wins is the team that scores more runs than the opponent. As far as cricket is concerned bowling amounts to being the dark side of the moon.

Let us conduct a simple experiment of replacing some of the team members Viv Richards played with during his time, with some members from the team Tendulkar was part of in the 1990s. Viv Richards is hailed, rightly, as a match winner. No sane person would challenge this. The question is: would he have been as great a match winner if instead of Malcolm Marshall, Michael Holding, Andy Roberts and Joel Garner, he had Javagal Srinath, Venkatesh Prasad, Venkatapathy Raju and Sunil Joshi bowling in his team? Let us throw in Kumble for Joshi later on. The blanket description of the West Indies fast bowlers as a quartet, hides the fact that these were four phenomenal individual all-time greats bowling at the same time. Similarly, take out Gordon Greenidge and Desmond Haynes as openers and replace them with Navjyot Sidhu and Ravi Shastri.

Then for good measure, let's drop Clive Lloyd and Jeffrey Dujon and replace them with Azharuddin and Nayan Mongia. Now let us reconsider the situation and ask these questions: How many matches would Viv Richards have won off his bat? How often would this team have beaten Australia in Australia? Would they have rolled over Ian Botham's Englishmen 5-0? Would they have won two World Cups?

Let us conduct a second experiment. The genesis of which lies in something that actually happened: Roger Federer, five-time Wimbledon champion, in a team situation. In 2002, Switzerland played Russia in the Davis Cup. The Swiss team included Roger Federer, Marc Rosset and Michel Kratochvil. The Russian team consisted of Marat Safin and Yevgeni Kafelnikov. Federer trounced Safin in straight sets (7-5, 6-1, 6-2) and dished out much the same treatment to Kafelnikov (7-6, 6-1, 6-1). But Kratochvil lost both his singles, and in the doubles, Federer and Rosset lost in four sets. Russia won 3-2.

Now imagine if Roger Federer was not in a three-man team but in an eleven-man team. Would his impact not have been diluted even further? Wouldn't the world champions then probably have been Spain or the US—the teams with the greatest overall bench strength? In this scenario, wouldn't we, in 2007, have hailed Rafael Nadal as perhaps a three- or four-time Wimbledon Champion—as part of an invincible Spanish armada? And what of Roger Federer? Perhaps we would say something like: 'There's no disputing his talent, but is he really a match winner?' Pete Sampras, another all-time tennis great, has a 762-222 singles record, but a losing 64-70 doubles record!

Add another real example: Tiger Woods, perhaps the best golfer and one of the best sportsmen *ever*, has one of the worst records *ever* in the Ryder Cup! The Ryder Cup is a team event, and Tiger wins when there is no team around him! Now imagine that Tiger was with ten Indian golfers in a team to compete in a World Cup comprising twelve teams. What odds would you give on his going to one final and two semi-finals (including the one where the team entered the final) out of five world cups?

Now let's look at the second aspect: the lack of real understanding about the importance of bowling. It is not insignificant that in the recent IPL auction all the designated icons were batsmen. The failure to find and develop bowlers who could take twenty wickets in a Test, or even defend a score of 300 in an ODI, is the cross that Sachin has had to bear.

Table I: Indian Team batting and bowling performances, Tests, 1990–May 2008

	1 January 1990–31 December 1999	*1 January 2000–9 May 2008*
Home		
Batting average	39.12	37.51
Bowling average	26.53	34.15
Away		
Batting average	32.90	36.71
Bowling average	40.97	36.10
Total		
Batting average	35.46	37.05
Bowling average	34.00	35.23

Firstly, Table I shows that the Indian team's overall batting average got better after 2000 (37.05) compared to the 1990s (35.46). This difference has been entirely driven by performances away from home; in fact, at home, the average has declined slightly. For those thinking, what is so big about a four-point difference (from 32.90 to 36.71), well, the difference is eighty runs over two completed innings in a Test (there are two innings of ten wickets for the entire team which means 20 wickets x 4 average points = 80), which surely is a significant factor. Secondly, and more significantly, the Indian bowlers' away performance has improved by almost five points—a remarkable improvement.

What this has led to in terms of match results is as follows:

Table II: Indian Team win/loss ratio, Tests, January 1990–May 2008

	1 January 1990–31 December 1999	1 January 2000–9 May 2008
Home		
Win	17	16
Loss	5	8
Draw	8	14
Win/Loss ratio	3.4:1	2:1
Away		
Win	1	17
Loss	15	17
Draw	23	16
Win/Loss ratio	0.06:1	1:1
Total		
Win	18	33
Loss	20	25
Draw	31	30
Win/Loss ratio	0.90:1	1.32

The table shows that we have reversed the win-loss ratio, by recording more victories than defeats. More importantly, it has transformed India from being a home team bully into a team that can win across conditions.

We will look at why this happened, in both batting and bowling terms.

In batting, the overall bench strength has significantly increased; and the away performances, too, have improved remarkably.

Table III: A Powerful Line-up Versus a One-man Army

From 1 January 2000 to May 2008: Test Average of India's 'Golden Indian Batting Generation'			*January 1990 to December 1999: Sachin in the company of the era's other batting stalwarts*		
	Home	Away		Home	Away
Sachin	51	57	Sachin	60	57
Dravid	55	58	Azhar	54	38
Ganguly	38	41	Sidhu	60	33
Laxman	51	47			
Sehwag	55	49			

In the current decade, we have had five batsmen who average more than forty away from home. In contrast, in the 1990s, we had just one: Sachin. Dravid, Ganguly and Laxman came into the team in the second half of the 1990s. But even with them in the team, in key encounters, like in 1999–2000 against Australia in Australia, Sachin was the lone ranger. Is there any surprise then why Sachin could not win much on tours in the 1990s? Or, why with the 'Golden Indian Batting Generation'—the best batting combination in Indian cricketing history—we have won much more? At home in the 1990s, there were three batsmen at least (and the occasional batsman like Kambli) who were strong, and our pitches were tailor-made for our spinners.

Let us look at the bowlers.

Table IV: India Bowlers, Test Averages, January 1990 to December 1999, and January 2000 to May 2008

	India bowlers from 1 January 2000 to May 2008			India bowlers from 1 January 1990 to 31 December 1999	
	Home	Away		Home	Away
Kumble	26.86	33.65	Srinath	24.88	35.01
Zaheer	40.09	31.46	Kumble	21.35	38.21
Harbhajan	25.34	42.48	Prasad	27.48	37.22
S. Sreesanth	38.84	28.86	Harbhajan	38.84	38.12
R.P. Singh		33.22			

What happened in Indian bowling, to cut a long story short, is that Kumble learnt to bowl well abroad, cutting his bowling average by five points and improving his strike rate from 92 to 61 (he actually went backwards at home but that has been partly covered up by Harbhajan). Then we discovered a new generation of fast bowlers, starting with Zaheer Khan, and including rookies like Sreesanth, R.P. Singh, and now Ishant Sharma, who are more comfortable bowling in away tours than their predecessors were and who have begun to exploit home pitches better than ever before.

The purpose of all this information is to put into context that, in his early years in international cricket, Sachin was playing with a team that was strong at home, but extremely weak away, and that post-2000, he has been in a more balanced team, which is capable of performing both at home and abroad.

We will use a religious analogy to summarize the situation. Like most people, we sometimes speculate on how to resolve the conundrum that if God exists, and is both all-loving and all-powerful, how come terrible things happen in life? Zoroaster, the prophet who founded Zoroastrianism, suggested a resolution to the puzzle. He opined that God is, and will always be, all-loving, but He is not yet all-powerful. Human beings have a key part to play (in the battle between God and the Devil)—to choose between good and evil. Unfortunately, there are people who choose evil. Zoroaster believed that good human beings will ultimately win one day against the evil lot, and on that day God will be all-powerful. We appreciate the concept: it does not put all the responsibility for winning on God but on the surrounding humans. Even for a cricketing God, to win with ten ordinary team-mates in a game like cricket is very hard. And for this cricket God to win, with some of the players not even interested in winning, is even tougher!

The Second Pillar: The Credibility of the Prosecution

Normally, the counsels for the defence cross-examine the weak witnesses so that their job is easier. But we will ask for the strongest witnesses. We will not waste time with the riff-raff who have complained or written against Sachin. We shall confine our cross-examination to *Wisden*, which some call 'The Cricket Bible', and Cricinfo, the cricket website (and now a magazine too). To put things in context, it has to be said that we read Cricinfo every day. Almost all the data we have shown in the book have been derived from Cricinfo's 'Statsguru'. We rate it as one of the best and most credible sources of cricket information and knowledge. Yet, for some reasons beyond our understanding, Cricinfo (via many writers) has time and again accused Sachin harshly.

In the Indian ethos it is perfectly fine to criticize God. There is a story of Nakeeran, a legendary Tamil poet, who debated with Shiva on a point of literature. He said, 'Even though it is you (Shiva) that I am debating with and even when you open your third eye and burn me to ash, I will defend what I have said about your poem because what is wrong is wrong.' In Indian mythology, gods can be mortal too. We have no issues with harsh criticism against Sachin when it is right. For example, as we mentioned in an earlier chapter, Sambit Bal, the chief editor of Cricinfo, wrote an article 'Watching Tendulkar was Embarrassing', on Sachin's batting on the fourth day of the third Test against South Africa in 2006–07. It was a strong critique of the maestro's approach in that innings. We appreciate and respect such writing.

We have five specific problems with Cricinfo from late 2006 to this date. We believe that there seems to be an orchestrated intent on the part of Cricinfo writers to show Sachin in a bad light. These are our points:

1. When Sachin was not doing well in this period, the criticism was brutal and eloquent. But when he was doing well, the coverage was 'correct' but muted and unenthusiastic. This is not fair.
2. The criticism has been based on a narrow time period and with caveats just to make a point against Sachin. A classic example is an article of 4 April 2007, written by S. Rajesh, titled 'The Real Culprits'. It opens with the caveat that India's batting woes during the period stemmed from a

failure to play on overseas tracks. The analysis covered the period September 2005 to April 2007, i.e., less than two years of Sachin's career of nearly two decades. Later, we will delve deeper on the data of Indian batsmen against the toughest opponent.
3. Moving on to relative judgements, when there have been two seemingly similar batsmen, Cricinfo has overrated other batsmen vis-à-vis Sachin even when it was clear that Sachin was better. For example, in an article entitled 'What to do with the Big Three?' (11 October 2007), in the content of ODIs, Sambit Bal wrote, 'Tendulkar is a batsman of a lifetime and Dravid isn't far behind.'
4. Such criticism has been incessant, as if waiting for half a chance.
5. When Sachin returned to form there were no apologies, or even acknowledgement that the criticism, based on narrow time periods with caveats during his dark period, was temporary and that he has proven them wrong. For example, Rajesh, after he published the article on 4 April 2007, has not since written on Sachin's fantastic batting overseas against South Africa, England and Australia.

Let us take up *Wisden*. The case against Sachin is that he has not featured in *Wisden*'s top 100 innings in Test matches (published in 2001). Many fans have shredded this list to pieces with great analysis; for instance, according to *Wisden*, Lara's fourth-innings 153 not out in Bridgetown in 1998–99 is the second-best innings ever, while Sachin's epic fourth-innings 136 in Madras in 1999 against Pakistan does not even feature in the top 100. Neither does his innings of 155 not out versus Australia in 1998, which turned around a match in which India had conceded a first innings lead.

Let us point out some more anomalies in the *Wisden* listings. To make it easier for the reader, we will take the same batsman, Tendulkar, who has got four innings in the top hundred of *Wisden*'s ODI list and look at the rating of two of these innings at the same venue (Sharjah) in the same year (1998): Sachin's 124 not out versus Zimbabwe is ranked at number 30 while his 134 against Australia in the final is rated at number 33! And believe it or not, his 143 versus Australia (out of a team total of 250, the famous 'post-sandstorm' century with which we qualified for the final of the Coca-Cola Cup) doesn't even feature in the top hundred! There are lists, and there are lists. Whatever criteria *Wisden* used, in our humble opinion, a winning century against the world's best team in a final is much more valuable than a winning century versus Zimbabwe. So you decide on the credibility of *Wisden*'s list.

This is not the end of the *Wisden* story. In late 2002, it published the greatest batsmen ever list.

Table V: *Wisden*'s Top Ten Batsmen Ever, till 2002

Ranking	Test Batsmen	ODI Batsmen
1	D.G. Bradman	I.V.A. Richards
2	S.R. Tendulkar	S.R. Tendulkar
3	I.V.A. Richards	B.C. Lara
4	G.S.A. Sobers	D. Jones
5	A.R. Border	M. Bevan
6	Jack Hobbs	S.C. Ganguly
7	K. Barrington	M. Waugh
8	S.M. Gavaskar	Z. Abbas
9	G.S. Chappell	J. Kallis
10	B.C. Lara	S. Anwar

In summary, Sachin, the second-best Test batsman (after the Don), by *Wisden*'s own reckoning, does not find a place in the list of the top hundred Test innings. Is this a case of the right hand not knowing what the left hand is doing, or a case of belated wisdom dawning upon Wisden? We won't speculate; you judge.

Let us now take up the credentials of another testimony. Ian Chappell, commentating in the final of the ODI CB triangular series in Australia involving Australia, India and Sri Lanka in 2008, said, 'Sachin has not done much for helping India to win against Australia unlike Lara has, particularly in the big games like a final, which is what Lara has done.' The fact is that Lara has never won a final against Australia! And, in contrast, Sachin has won three finals against the world's best team with scores of 134 in 1998 in Sharjah (man of the match), 117 not out in 2008 in Sydney (man of the match) and 91 in 2008 in Brisbane (top scorer).

Writing on the issue of selecting the big three—Tendulkar, Ganguly and Dravid—for ODIs, Sambit Bal wrote on 10 October 2007 that though they still had plenty to offer, they needed to be phased out gradually for the sake of the team's future. Bal went on to say, 'Tendulkar is a batsman of a lifetime and Dravid isn't far behind.' Is Dravid really not 'far behind'? Dravid has never won a single man of the series while Sachin has won thirteen, including in World Cup 2003, Dravid has not won a single man of the match award in a World Cup match while Sachin has won eight, and Dravid has not won a single man of the match in an ODI against Australia while Sachin has won nine.

Such are the analyses of the witnesses and accusers!

The Third Pillar: The Specific Charges

Accusation 1: Sachin Tendulkar is not a match winner: In the context of ODIs, the charge is so absurd that it would be a complete waste of the court's time to even consider the case. Let us start with the broad figures: 16,361 runs at an average of 44.33 and a strike rate of 85.49 with 42 centuries and 89 fifties, an average of over 35 against all the 15 opponents, except South Africa (32) and Ireland (just one match), an average of over 35 in every one of the sixteen countries he has played, except New Zealand (30). Let us now look at some tables which speak louder than all the prosecution witnesses.

Table VI: Sachin, ODI performance by venue

	Home	*Away*	*Neutral*
Runs	5766	4446	6149
Average	46.12	36.44	50.40
Strike Rate	86.98	80.76	87.80
Centuries	16	9	17
Fifties	33	23	33

Table VII: Sachin, ODI performance, matches won

December 1989 to May 2008	*Home*	*Away*	*Neutral*	*Total*
Matches won	82	52	72	206
Sachin's Average	52.55	50.31	69.41	57.43
Man of the Match	20	9	28	57

Table VIII: India ODI performance, with Sachin playing and not playing

December 1989 to May 2008	Won	Lost	No result / tie
Sachin played	206	186	25
Sachin didn't play	46	51	3
Total	252	237	28

It is clear that when Sachin plays the team wins more often than it loses, but when he has not played, India has lost more than it has won. The exact win-loss ratio drops from 1.1 with Sachin to 0.9 without Sachin. When India has won, Sachin's average and strike rate have been significantly high. We will conclude by saying he is a match winner for the team, which would have lost more matches than won if he weren't playing.

Now, let us look at Tests. Sachin's record at home in Test matches is exemplary. For example, in an entire decade (1990s) of home Test matches, India won six series, drew three, and recorded three 'one-off Test' wins. No losses at all. Then India was truly the final frontier; Sachin's batting average during this period was 59.88. We rest our case. Let's now turn to the away Tests debate.

We have already established that during the 1990s the Indian bowling attack was conceding 2.88 runs per over and also conceding 40.97 runs per wicket. Let us round this off to forty runs per wicket and three runs per over. To concede about forty runs, which is what we needed to do to get a wicket, we would need thirteen overs at three runs per over ($13 \times 3 = 39$). That means to take twenty wickets, it took 260 overs (13 overs per wicket $\times$ 20 wickets), thereby almost ruling out any chance of a win in a 450-over Test (assuming 90 overs per day and five completed days). The reality, using the actual numbers and not these approximations, is closer to 280 overs. Now try getting the batsmen to score in 170 overs (450 less 280) what the opposition has scored in 280!

But this is theoretical. Let us get to what actually happened. Let us reconstruct the events of that decade of the 1990s.

India played 39 Tests away in the 1990s. Any ideas as to how many times Indian bowlers took twenty wickets in these Tests? A mere six times in a decade of away Tests. So, in theory, Sachin had six opportunities to win a Test in a decade of away cricket. Of these, India won one and Sachin got 104 not out in Sri Lanka in that Test. Let's go into the details of the remaining five such Tests. India had to chase 372 in the fourth innings in Adelaide against Craig McDermott/Merv Hughes/Mike Whitney. Could we have got to 372? The answer, surprisingly, is 'yes', because we got to 333. This is one possible near-miss, but the odds of chasing 372 on the fifth day are never particularly high. The second occasion was in Johannesburg, November 1992. Sachin got 111 in this match but it ended in a draw. In the third at Durban, December 1996, India were all out for 100 and 66 in the two innings. Not much chance of a victory there. The fourth was a loss, chasing 120 in the fourth innings at Barbados, March 1997. Sachin got 92 and 4 in the match. Perhaps he should have got a fifty in the second as well! Finally, we failed to get 235 at Harare against Zimbabwe in October 1998. To put it bluntly, when India had six chances to win, Sachin got a 100 or near-hundred in three of these, i.e., he created a conversion opportunity in 50 per cent of the Tests we had a theoretical opportunity of winning. Imagine, now, being in a team with a backup like Clive Lloyd, Gordon Greenidge, Dujon and

Haynes! How many of the three centuries/near centuries would have been converted to wins, even excluding the upside of having Marshall/Garner/Holding and Roberts!

Don't just ask what God was doing; also ask what the ten humans were doing in these matches!

After 2000, the era of away wins started: remember, our winning ratio changed from 0.06:1 to 1:1. We have explained how the team with five strong batsmen and a balanced bowling attack created so many more opportunities to win. India won 17 Tests out of the 50 played overseas since 2000. Of these, Sachin Tendulkar played in 13 and averaged 87.40 in the wins. Let us exclude victories against Bangladesh (four) and Zimbabwe (one). His average is still a healthy 64.75.

Let us go into each of the eight major Test wins against Australia (two), England (two), Pakistan (two), South Africa (one) and West Indies (one). We will assess Sachin's contribution in each and provide the supporting facts alongside.

Table IX: Sachin's Contribution in India's Major Test Wins after 2000

	Sachin's Contribution	*Our Assessment*
Adelaide 2003	1 & 37; 2/36 (Martyn 38 and Waugh 42)	Useful, from a bowling standpoint, as Martyn and Waugh were staging a revival. But the major contributors were Dravid (over 300 runs) and Agarkar. Also, Sachin's 37 while chasing 235 to win was useful.

Continued

Continued

	Sachin's Contribution	*Our Assessment*
Perth 2008	71 & 13	Significant. Turned the match around from 59/2 in the first innings
Leeds 2002	193 (top score)	Outstanding contribution
Nottingham 2007	91 (top score) & 1	Outstanding contribution—held the innings together
Multan 2004	194 not out & 2/36	Outstanding contribution. Match remembered more for Sehwag's incandescent 309 off just 375 balls.
Rawalpindi 2004	1 and 1 wicket	Insignificant
Johannesburg 2007	44 out of a team total of 284 on a green top.	Significant. India was 14 for 2 when Sachin walked in. One more wicket could have led to collapse as this was a wicket in which South Africa was bowled out for 84!
Trinidad 2002	117 (top score) and 0	Outstanding. Margin of win was 37 runs.

Out of the eight wins, we rate his contribution as outstanding in four, significant in two, useful in one and insignificant in one. This detailed assessment on away wins against major Test-playing nations comprehensively answers the question whether Sachin is a match winner in away Tests or not.

Accusation 2: Sachin's record in ODI finals: We will talk about this in the overall career context later. Here let us limit ourselves to a set of stats concerning the period 4 April 1999 to 6 September 2005 when India played twenty-one ODI finals.

It is true to say that with a God in their midst, India should have won more than one out of the twenty-one finals. However, the reality is that the God was not amidst them for all of the twenty-one games, due to injuries. Sachin did not play in seven; of the remaining fourteen, three were either not completed or were washed out. That leaves eleven games to start with, i.e., about half the issue on hand! In these eleven games, we admit that Sachin's average of 23 was well below his overall record in finals. In fact, when you look at the 'tennis elbow' and the injuries-bound phase, and compare it with his overall career, the correct conclusion is that for India to win an ODI final, Sachin had to play a massive hand (the NatWest final versus England in July 2002 was an exception, with Sachin getting just 14 as India overcame all odds to successfully chase 325 after being 146 for 5 at one stage).

Of these eleven games four are of particular interest. Two of them are the big finals: World Cup 2003 and ICC Knockout 2000. In the World Cup final, India got a hiding when its fast bowlers failed miserably on a track that was initially helpful to bowlers. The Indians had to chase a near-impossible target of 360 against Australia. Tendulkar went in the first over itself slogging against McGrath, and India's number was pretty much up after its first fifteen overs. The second big match was the ICC Knockout final in 2000. In this match, Sachin hit 69 runs off 83 balls in an opening stand of 141 in 26 overs with Ganguly. Yet the team folded up for 264—and there was no Shane Bond either. Sachin also bowled well in that match with 1/38 from 10 overs. Would we be hailing Viv Richards for a match-winning contribution if he had got 69 runs and 1/38?

Absolutely! Because the batsmen following him would have closed out the game with a 300-plus total, and his bowlers would have defended it easily. This is the broader context of cricket being a team game. The third match of interest is the final against Australia in 2004 in Calcutta. Chasing 235, India was bowled out for 198. Sachin got 45 off 66 balls, but six of the Indian players got out for five or less. Sachin learnt from this experience while playing in Australia in 2008, and he realized that he would have to do it all himself! The final match of interest is against Sri Lanka in Colombo in 2004. Sri Lanka put on 228 and India were able to get only 203/9 in reply. Sachin got 74 runs off 100 balls and took 2/40 from his 10 overs. (Zaheer Khan was the next highest scorer with 28 runs.) Would this have been a match-winning performance for Viv Richards with his support cast? Absolutely!

What we are trying to convey is that even in the worst phase of his career—when he was plagued by tendonitis—Sachin put up potentially match-winning performances in two out of eleven finals; in one other, he gave the team a 50-50 chance. Our defence is that had Richards or Ponting put in an equivalent performance in those three finals, the game would have been closed out by their team-mates. In Sachin's case he has to start, consolidate and finish off the game, because the rest have the capacity to lose a game from any situation. We rave about the Natwest Trophy win because it was a great effort, chasing 325. We can also say that it was one ODI final we remember well because India won without Sachin's help in all these years!

Accusations 3 and 4: Tendulkar plays for statistics and not for the team and has changed his natural game: Since these two charges are related, let us deal with them together. Ian Chappell's specific statement is at the crux of this charge: '...he looks like a player trying to eke out a career; build on a glittering array of statistics.' Surely, there is some anomaly about using the words 'eke out' and 'glittering statistics' in the same breath? You can either struggle or glitter, but not both. But the reality is that Sachin's strike rate in both Tests and ODIs has been very good consistently. So he has not been 'eking' out runs but scoring them at a good pace. There is an impression that he is batting slower than when he was a teenager. We often hear people saying, 'Why can't Sachin bat as if he was sixteen again or twenty again?' Please take a look at the numbers!

Table X: Sachin, year-wise strike rate

	Tests	*ODIs*
Career strike rate	54	85
1989	44	NA
1990	48*	98
1991	39	74
1992	56	69
1993	48	73
1994	59	88
1995	58	101
1996	48	82
1997	56	85
1998	50	102
1999	75	88
2000	60	81
2001	57	91
2002	54	87

Continued

Continued

	Tests	ODIs
2003	39	87
2004	56	80
2005	44	77
2006	53	77
2007	52	85
2008 (up to 9 May)	63	85

Note: Test strike rate for 1990: One innings has not been considered as number of balls faced is unavailable.

The mistake Chappell and Cricinfo statisticians make on a regular basis is to draw big conclusions from small data samples. The dangers of looking at non-representative samples are well known to statisticians in the business field. Hence considerable effort is made by research companies to get sample sizes and sample 'representativeness' right. An error in sampling leads to a conclusion which is at best limited and, at worst, invalid.

For example, talking about a young Sachin's first innings as an opener in ODIs against New Zealand (March 1994, 82 runs off 49 balls) in the light of his Test innings against South Africa at Cape Town (14 runs off 62 balls in January 2007) is like creating a database which is statistically too small, not reliable and not valid. And therefore incorrect!

Accusation 5: Sachin has not yet played a Test knock that can find a place in Wisden's top 100 Test knocks: We have covered this earlier. We close this subject with a thought: the fact that Mahatma Gandhi did not win a Nobel Peace Prize is not Gandhi's loss; it is the Nobel Academy's loss.

Accusation 6: Sachin has not led India to victory in any famous fourth-innings chase: To us this is like evaluating a footballer on the basis of how many games he has won by scoring a goal in the last five minutes of the game! We prefer footballers who make sure their teams go two-up at half time so that the last five minutes are less exciting! We don't know if Michael Jordan is assessed on how many points he scores or on the assists he makes in the last quarter; or if Maradona is assessed on performance in the first as against the second half of a game. In Test cricket, each of the four innings is important, and there is always a different way to contribute to the team. Personally, we like the third innings of Tests because some famous Indian wins have been tailored there. Think of the third innings in 1974 in Calcutta versus the West Indies or the Madras Test versus Australia in 1998. In the former, India, 7 runs behind in the first innings, put on 316 in its second innings (the third innings of the match) inclusive of a great 139 from G.R. Viswanath, eventually winning the Test by 85 runs with Bedi and Chandra taking seven wickets in the last innings. In March 1998, in Madras, India conceded a 71-run lead in the first innings but went on to put up 418 for 4 in the second innings driven by Sachin's 155 not out. Kumble, V. Raju and Rajesh Chauhan then wrapped up Australia for 168 runs giving India a 179-run victory. And of course, there is the Indian second innings (the third innings of the match) in 2001 in Calcutta versus Australia where India came back from the dead after following-on to register what is beyond doubt India's greatest Test victory!

Let us also remember some of Sachin's important fourth innings. As a seventeen-year-old, he saved a Test against England (scoring 119 not out at Manchester in 1990) and won the man of the match; he was awarded a champagne bottle and GBP 500.

Some argued later that it might have been improper to award a champagne bottle to a minor! We have talked about the small but important 37 that he made in Adelaide. Recently, in 2007, he ended at 56 not out when India won against Pakistan in Delhi. Of course, who can forget his epic 136 against Pakistan in 1999 in Madras? This particular innings again underlines the value of the support cast, and asserts that cricket is a team game. Look closely at the scorecard of the West Indies innings when Lara made 153 not out against Australia at Bridgetown in March 1999 and you will find that he got help from Curtly Ambrose and up the order from the openers. Ponting's fourth-innings century in the 2005 Ashes series made him a hero for saving a Test, but he was helped by the last pair who stayed for twenty-four balls. In contrast, see what happened in Madras 1999: barring Mongia's 52, no one else crossed 10; numbers nine, ten and Jack made a grand total of two runs! The remaining batsmen scored 24 runs in 143 balls at a strike rate of one run per over! Had the rest of the top-order batsmen scored even at 1.5 runs per over, it would have been sufficient for India to win.

Accusation 7: Sachin's Test average is good because of 'not outs': We don't know how to respond to this one! If we take every innings played whether not out or out as a completed innings and divide the runs scored in total by the number of innings played, Sachin's average is 49.5 vis-à-vis Lara's 51, Richards's 47, Ponting's 51 and Dravid's 48 (as of 9 May 2008). It is of interest that out of Bradman's 80 innings, 10 were unbeaten—that is, he has remained unbeaten 12.5 per cent overall. By the same token, Bradman's average goes down to the eighties—far below the near-magical 100. Finally, one can't accuse a batsman for being 'not out' and for not 'being there till the end' in the same breath.

Accusation 8: Tendulkar's performance against top opposition is lukewarm: This is an interesting one. It is based on the premise that the best players always like to measure themselves against the strongest opposition, and in Tendulkar's case the recent numbers don't stack up well at all.

Rajesh's data, of course, goes on to imply that Kaif, in the period under consideration, is India's leading batsman on tough wickets, and not Sachin and Dravid, who are, by implication, flat-track bullies. This is the kind of analysis that extrapolates a mountain out of a statistical molehill. Let us look at this point with the fullness of data and in perspective. The reality is that against the best players and the strongest opposition, Sachin's numbers clinch the case.

The Case for Sachin

We could have started this in many ways. Some people say that fans use flowery language to praise him without any data. Sachin is indeed beyond numbers, but his stats are the foundation for his case. And we want to sift the data to conclude whether the critics' case against Sachin is robust or rubbish.

So let us start with the overall record. Tests: 11,782 runs at an average of 55.31, with 39 centuries and 49 fifties; an average of above 40 against all opponents except South Africa (35); an average of above 40 in every one of the ten countries he has played in; a very well-balanced home-versus-away record on average—55 and 56, respectively; in the case of total runs and centuries, higher numbers away (6726 and 23) than home (5056 and 16). ODIs: 16,361 runs at an average of 44.33 and a strike rate of 85.49, with 42 centuries and 89 fifties; an average of above 35 against all the fifteen opponents, except South Africa

(32) and Ireland (just one match); an average of above 35 in each one of the sixteen countries he has played in except New Zealand (30).

As for records in international cricket, the stats are staggering: highest runs, centuries, man of the match awards, man of the series awards.... For most, such figures by themselves are enough to make him the greatest batsmen after Bradman. However, for some like Ian Chappell, 'Sachin is only collecting glittering stats now.' The devil's advocates have identified what in their view are his weaknesses. We will delve with deep analysis to judge if they are true.

We won't waste time showcasing Sachin's record against Bangladesh. We will show you Sachin's records (in comparison to his contemporaries) against Australia, by a mile the number one team right through the 1990s and in the new millennium. The data in Table XI include the figures of batsmen who made up India's 'Golden Batting Generation', two other Indians who were the support cast in the 1990s, and two batsmen each from other countries, in Test matches.

Table XI: Sachin versus the rest: Performance against and in Australia

Player	Overall Career Average	Average vs Australia	Average in Australia (i.e. 'away')
S.R. Tendulkar	56	**56**	59
V. Sehwag	50	**54**	60
K.P. Pietersen	50	**54**	54
V.V.S. Laxman	44	**51**	54
B.C. Lara	53	**51**	42

Player	Overall Career Average	Average vs Australia	Average in Australia (i.e. 'away')
Martin Crowe	45	**48**	67
A. de Silva	43	**47**	38
Rahul Dravid	55	**46**	49
N.S. Sidhu	42	**44**	20
M. Azharuddin	45	**39**	28
Jacques Kallis	58	**38**	49
S. Chanderpaul	47	**35**	32
Graham Gooch	43	**33**	33
Sourav Ganguly	42	**32**	35
Inzamam-ul Haq	50	**31**	31
S. Jayasuriya	40	**31**	31
M. Yousuf	55	**30**	33
Stephen Fleming	40	**25**	29
G. Smith	47	**22**	21

The first thing that is striking about Table XI is that among the top five—with an average of above fifty against Australia—three are Indians from its 'Golden Batting Generation'; moreover, all the three have higher averages versus Australia than their respective career averages (note: Sachin's career average is 55.5, while it is 56.00 versus Australia). Furthermore, if we also consider Dravid's and Ganguly's numbers, we find that all the five have higher away averages than at home. Now look at the contrast with players of other teams either versus Australia or in Australia, or both. For example, even the great Lara has a slightly lower average against Australia than his career average; and his average in Australia (i.e. away) is significantly lower. If anyone doesn't understand why the Aussies are worried about

India in Test matches, the above table should be an eye-opener. Also, those who cannot fathom why Sachin didn't win away games in the 1990s should look at the data on his support cast's (Azhar's and Sidhu's) away record. And then look again at our bowlers in away matches (Table I). Finally, while the Aussies are well aware about India's Test history and its strengths and they fear it, Indians have little memory: India committed the cardinal sin of not selecting Sehwag in the first two Tests (especially the Boxing Day Test) in the 2007–08 series. Just look at his record against Australia! Opening with Sehwag could have changed the series.

Statistics is more true than false, and the stat called 'average' is an important measure, more important than what some people think! Before we get to who has been the best batsman against Australia in the 1990s and in the early twenty-first century, we need to assess other factors: number of centuries, kind of contributions made to the team, the desire and hard work needed to win (the result itself is a different thing—always remember Sydney 2008), special knocks (like Laxman's 281, Dravid's 233, Lara's 153 not out, Sachin's 155 not out, Sehwag's 195, etc.). One of the key factors is consistency, series after series. Kevin Pietersen has played only two series against Australia so far and Sehwag has played three. However, our gut feeling is that they will be in the top few even after many series. Let's compare and contrast the series by series record of three Indian batsmen to illustrate the consistency factor.

Dravid had a good start against Australia in 1998 at home with three half-centuries following the customary failures in his home ground at Bangalore. Then, just as most people thought he would shine in his second series, his away scores in 1999–2000 were pathetic: 35, 6; 9, 14; 29, 0; a total of 93 runs in the series. His third series (home in 2001) started with three failures, and by then the experts had started questioning his ability against a tough Australian side. But then came that magical 180 in Calcutta. That innings alone made his series; we don't need any other data about that series. His fourth series against Australia was his peak, his hour of glory. Against this background, i.e., when he was it his peak, and with Sachin out due to 'tennis elbow' (and Ganguly, too, out due to injury), the whole of India looked up to him in the home series in 2004, to win or at least to draw it so that the 'last frontier' would not be conquered by the Aussies. And what did he do? Starting with a duck at his home ground, he made a total of 109 runs in the first three Tests of a four-Test series. By the time we got to Bombay for the last Test, the 'last frontier' had been lost with Australia up 2-0. For perspective, Sehwag made 155 in just one innings in Madras, a match we could have won but for rain on the fifth day. Dravid did score 31 not out and 27 in a very low-scoring match in Bombay, which gave India a consolation win. Overall, the series was a personal disappointment indeed. Dravid's sixth series against Australia (in 2007–08) was as inconsistent as has been his overall record against Australia. Sheer agony in Melbourne (starting with 5 runs off 66 balls with an 'out off a no ball' and a dropped catch to boot), fighting knocks in Sydney (we really admired his spirit in contrast to Yuvi's attitude), playing a very important hand in a winning team effort in Perth, and ending the series on an unfortunate note with a broken finger after a failure in the first innings.

Laxman started with a 95 in Calcutta in 1998 in a match that India won. In his second series against Australia (1999–2000, away), Laxman started badly. And then came the blinder (167) in Sydney out of the team's total of 267. In his third series against the Aussies (2001 at home), he made 59 in Calcutta in the first innings, following it up with the monumental 281 in the second innings. He continued well in Madras, too. In the away series in 2003–04, while Dravid was deservedly the man of the series, it was Laxman who foiled the Aussies, combining successfully with a different Indian batsman in each Test (Ganguly in Brisbane, Sehwag in Melbourne, Dravid in Adelaide, and Sachin in Sydney). And then the string of high performances was broken, and how! At home in 2004, he failed miserably in the first three Tests, managing only 53 runs. With Sachin injured, and Dravid and Laxman failing, it was no surprise that we lost the series. In the final Test of the series in Bombay, Laxman made a very important second-innings fifty. In the 2007–08 away series, Laxman started with 26 and 42 in Melbourne—too few to help the team. But then he went on to smash a glorious century in Sydney, which he seems to own along with Sachin! In Perth, Laxman's second-innings 79 was critical to the memorable Indian victory. Playing perhaps his last innings on Australian soil in the fourth Test of the series at Adelaide, he scored 51 in the first innings.

Sachin played his first series against the Aussies at the age of eighteen. He cracked two centuries—in Sydney and Perth. The former was a masterpiece; Richie Benaud rated it as the best century made by a non-Australian on Australian soil. His second series against Australia in 1998 at home was billed as the 'Sachin vs. Warne' battle. The battle was won even before the Test series started, with Sachin scoring a winning double century for Bombay (yes, the Ranji team beat the mighty Aussies). Tendulkar reconfirmed it with the legendary second-innings 155 not out in Madras, 79 in Calcutta and 177 in Bangalore; he was awarded the man of the series title for his efforts. This was India's first-ever series victory over a full-strength Australian team (we discount the victory achieved against what we call an Australian 'B team', under Kim Hughes in 1979, which was without the big players who were playing for Kerry Packer). In Sachin's third series (away, 1999–2000), the team let him down badly; but he, as usual, stood tall—man of the series again. In the 2001 series at home, Sachin scored a half century in each innings in Bombay while others were struggling. Although Calcutta was the Laxman–Dravid–Bhajji show, and though he failed with the bat, Sachin took three important wickets after tea on the fifth day as India came back from the dead to record its greatest Test victory. And then came his customary Madras century, which sealed India's famous series win. In the away series of 2003–04, Sachin was not his normal self. Still, in the Adelaide victory, he took two important second-innings wickets. Of course Sachin could not have finished a series without leaving a mark—so there were the 241 not out and 60 not out in Sydney, which ought to have given us a series win. In 2004 (at home) he was desperate to play, but he simply could not in Bangalore and Madras. We feel that he was rushed to play from the third Test because India was down 0-1. His elbow had not totally healed, and on hindsight it proved to be a bad decision since he needed a second operation later. Still, Sachin Ramesh Tendulkar could not close a series against Australia without something significant. His brilliant counter attacking second-innings half century with Laxman gave India hope, and Murali Karthik fashioned a consolation win in Bombay. The 2004 home series showed in some ways how pivotal Sachin has been for the team. Then came the 2007–08 series—most likely a memorable farewell to Australia. He scored 493 runs at an average of 70, with two half-centuries, and two scores above 150, to effectively silence Ian Chappell, who wrote that 'Mirror, mirror' article in Cricinfo. Sachin plundered 62 in Melbourne while the rest were scratching for runs, he stroked a statesman-like 154 not out in Sydney, an audacious 71 in Perth and a delectable 153 in Adelaide, which was a summation of the series, of his batting against Australia in his career, and much more.

This is the kind of series-by-series consistency over a period of sixteen years that Tendulkar has achieved against the best team in the world, which rightly puts him in the bracket of a champion performer.

We now turn to Sachin's ODI record against Australia. We start with the utter nonsense about the 'The Big Three in One Day Cricket'—Tendulkar, Dravid and Ganguly, according to Cricinfo's Sambit Bal—as if they are all more or less equally good in ODIs. Thinking thus is akin to thinking that in aviation, first, business and economy classes are the same on fares, comfort, etc. We are unequivocal in our opinion that Sachin and Viv Richards are the top two ODI batsmen in history, Ganguly is the second-best Indian ODI batsman in history, and Dravid will not feature in our 'Top Five Indian ODI Batsmen'. Strictly speaking, in the realm of India's ODIs, we have only two all-time great batsmen (Tendulkar and Ganguly). We rate Dravid as one of the top Indian Test batsmen, along with Sachin, Gavaskar and G.R. Viswanath. Sehwag has the potential to break into that list.

Rajesh's article in Cricinfo titled 'The Real Culprits' (4 April 2007) makes a great, fundamental point about how well a player plays against the top opponents. The flaw with his article is that he takes a small set of data to draw a major conclusion. Taking the data from September 2005 to April 2007, one table demonstrates how good Kaif has been. Another table shows that Yuvraj has the highest average against Australia and South Africa (based on five matches played during this period), and Sachin (based on eleven matches he played against South Africa and Australia) finishes last among the six batsmen analysed. This is like saying, 'If Jack Hobbs batted well a few times on a sticky wicket for eleven matches in time frame X and in the same time frame, the Don averaged less, then Jack Hobbs is God and Donald Bradman is the worst culprit.' This almost tempts us to make an observation about statisticians: they come to a conclusion beforehand and then go about looking for the data to support it, no matter how small the data set may be. In business, there is a phenomenon called the 'recency syndrome', wherein the most recent information drives perceptions disproportionately. It seems that even the most rigorous statisticians are not immune to the 'recency syndrome'.

Ian Chappell argued that Sachin is collecting 'glittering statistics' but has little to show in terms of Indian wins. So we set about researching the data on India's ODI wins overall and wins against Australia, to compare how the so-called 'The Big Three' have performed. Of course, we had to add Kaif and Yuvi as it was our moral duty to debate with Rajesh by providing evidence. Then we added Azhar and Sidhu—the supporting cast of Indian batsmen in the 1990s. Finally, we added Lara because he and Sachin were similar in many ways, most importantly in that they were 'lone, great warriors' stuck in below-average teams against the most challenging of opponents. Our gut feeling was right directionally, but the magnitude turned out to be so right that we fell off our chairs.

What are the salient points from the data in Table XII on page 112?

1. It is normal that the average of a batsman when the team has won gets to be higher than his overall average, i.e., column three versus two. That is not a surprise.
2. We did think before this analysis that for West Indies to beat Australia, Lara was critical. But the stats turned out

Table XII: Contribution to winning matches

Player	Overall average and strike rate	Average and strike rate in matches won vs all teams	Matches won vs Australia	Average and strike rate in Matches won vs Australia	Man of the match in matches won vs Australia
Col 1	Col 2	Col 3	Col 4	Col 5	Col 6
Sachin Tendulkar	$44 \times 85 = 37$	$57 \times 90 = 51$	20	$78 \times 91 = 71$	9 (of 20)
Rahul Dravid	$39 \times 71 = 28$	$52 \times 76 = 40$	9	$37 \times 80 = 30$	0 (of 9)
Sourav Ganguly	$41 \times 74 = 30$	$55 \times 78 = 43$	10	$19 \times 59 = 11$	0 (of 10)
Md. Kaif	$32 \times 72 = 23$	$43 \times 75 = 32$	1	N.A.	0 (of 1)
Yuvraj Singh	$36 \times 87 = 31$	$49 \times 94 = 46$	8	$30 \times 88 = 26$	1 (of 8)
Md. Azharuddin	$37 \times 74 = 27$	$48 \times 80 = 38$	20	$36 \times 83 = 30$	3 (of 20)
N.S. Sidhu	$37 \times 70 = 26$	$52 \times 73 = 38$	6	$37 \times 70 = 26$	1 (of 6)
Brian Lara	$40 \times 80 = 32$	$62 \times 86 = 53$	18	$70 \times 83 = 58$	4 (of 18)

Note: We have used a measure we can call 'batting momentum'. Inspired by the measure in physics (momentum as mass multiplied by velocity), we use a measure of mass of runs (on average) multiplied by the speed with which they have been scored (strike rate), vectors ignored. Thus, for Sachin (Col 2), we have an average of 44 and a strike rate of 85 to give a momentum of 37 ($44 \times 85 = 3740$, which we round off to 37).

to be amazing. Lara had to raise his average to 70 runs to help his team win and has won the man of the match award in 22 per cent of the matches that his team won against Australia while he was playing.

3. Kaif has played in precisely one match when India has won against Australia, and he made 1 not out. In total, he has played against Australia in eight matches, and has made 71 runs at an average of 12. Let us understand this: the total runs that Kaif has made against Australia (irrespective of the result) are 71; Sachin has an average of 78 in matches when India has won against Australia! Yuvraj's average when India has won against Australia is lower than his overall average, including in matches that India has lost!

4. The averages of the rest of the support cast of the Indian batting in the last eighteen years are equally eye-opening: their contributions to an Indian win against Australia are less than their normal contribution to an Indian win. Only Sachin's match-winning contribution in a match versus Australia actually improves—he really has to do the heavy lifting against the best team.

5. Azhar has won three man of the match awards (i.e., he was the key player in victories); Yuvi and Sidhu have one each. Neither Dravid nor Ganguly has won a man of the match against Australia helping India to win.

Sachin's performance in matches that India has won is better than his overall average. But his performance in matches won versus Australia is stupendous with his career average going up from 44 to 78 and his strike rate from 85 to 91. These are the statistics, but he has done much more. What Sachin has done is to lift India as a team that could beat the champions in ODIs, just as he lifted India as a team that could register its first 'real' Test series win against Australia in 1998. Lara raised West Indies as a team to win against Australia—a magnificent feat—but not on the same scale as Sachin. Lara won the man of the match award in 22 per cent of the matches that West Indies won against Australia while he was playing. Overall, with or without Lara, before or after Lara, West Indies have won 57 matches (exactly 50 per cent of its matches against Australia, as of May 2008); and Lara's four man of the match awards constitute only seven per cent of West Indies' wins against Australia. In the 1970s and 1980s, West Indian victories over the Aussies were a regular affair.

Let us compare Lara's man of the match record to Sachin's. Sachin has won the man of the match award in 45 per cent of the matches that he has played when India has beaten Australia, i.e., almost half of all Indian wins he has played in and double that of Lara's figure in this aspect!

To sum up, India has won thirty-two ODIs against Australia ever since the format of the game started. Sachin has not only played in twenty of these, he has been player of the match nine times. Of the other eleven matches, Sachin has made useful to very significant contributions in nine: 36 and 4-0-8-0 in Perth, December 1991 (useful); 47 and 8-0-33-1 in Dunedin 1995 (useful); 62 in a 5-run win at Mohali in November 1996 (very significant); 38 of 37 balls and 7-0-31-1 in Nairobi, October 2001 (useful); 35 off 26 balls in Bangalore, March 2001 (useful); 86 in Brisbane, January 2004 (very significant); 79 in Chandigarh, October 2007 (significant); 44 in Melbourne, February 2008 (useful); 41 in Brisbane March 2008 (useful). Now we come to the two failures: 6 in Sharjah in April 1994 (but then he also bowled eight overs, giving away only 39 runs in an innings where Australia got 244—a par bowling performance from a part-time, fifth bowler), and 21 chasing 194 for a win when Uthappa and the tail-enders took us to a win. In short, nine man of the match performances and nine significant/useful performances in twenty matches. Does this look like a match winner or someone chasing 'glittering stats'? You decide!

We return to examine Ian Chappell's article further. We want to believe that the error Ian makes is in not understanding the context. Perhaps he did not think deeply enough about the context of an Australian team playing against a weak side that rode on one man's shoulders.

Let us examine some more data (see Table XIII).

Table XIII: Sachin and Lara versus Australia, and Australians versus India and West Indies

Player	Overall ODI average	Average in wins vs all teams	Matches won vs Australia or WI + India	Average in wins vs Australia or WI + India	Man of the Match won vs Australia or WI + India
Col 1	Col 2	Col 3	Col 4	Col 5	Col 6
Sachin Tendulkar	44	57	20	78	9 (of 20)
Brian Lara	40	62	18	70	4 (of 18)
Ricky Ponting	43	50	45	43	5 (of 45)
Matthew Hayden	45	46	21	50	3 (of 21)
Adam Gilchrist	36	41	41	39	5 (of 41)

Note: The objective is to show how the greats have done against each other to illustrate Lara's and Tendulkar's record against Australia. For Lara and Tendulkar we have used the statistics against Australia. For the Australians, we have used the statistics against Lara's and Tendulkar's teams, viz., West Indies and India which are summarized as WI + India in the table.

The information in Table XIII is very interesting indeed. Why is it that for Australia's top batsmen the averages in matches won are only slightly higher (column three vs two, or column five vs two) unlike the Indian batsman and Lara, whose averages in this case are significantly higher?

Well, to start with, the Australians win a lot, so their averages don't move much when you compare matches won with matches played, unlike other teams such as India whose win-loss ratio is roughly even. Going deeper, Australia's top batsmen have a great support cast in batting. And importantly, they convert their runs into wins by their great bowling and fielding, unlike India. For instance, in the crucial Nagpur match in 2007, with which Australia took a series-clinching fourth win in a seven-match series, Hayden did not play and Clarke made a duck, but Gilchrist made 51 and Ponting made 49—so in all, the first three batsmen made around hundred runs between them, which was useful but not a match-winning start. But despite the fact that the Indian batsmen did well (299), with Sachin scoring 72 off 72 balls and Ganguly making 84, we lost. Why? Because Andrew Symonds hammered a ton; on another day, it could have been Hussey or someone else. More importantly, Sreesanth dropped Symonds when he was batting on two.

Ian Chappell has not grasped the difference between the Australian context and a Sachin-powered Indian one or a Lara-powered West Indian team. When Australia bats, there are five or more batsmen in the team who can win the match. When India or West Indies try to win against Australia, the support cast in batting, and the overall bowling and fielding, range from average to poor. So, for Sachin or Lara to win against Australia, they have to make 70–78 runs on an average.

Put simply, if Sachin or Lara had been in the Australian team, they would have won a lot more than what they have done, and even achieved a lot more than what Ponting, Hayden and Gilchrist have. Secondly, if Ponting, Hayden or Gilchrist had been in the Indian or West Indian teams, they would have won a lot less than what they have done, and it is also likely that they would not have performed the way that Sachin and Lara have performed.

A lone great warrior burdened with ten ordinary players taking on a champion team and winning against it is an extraordinary feat. What Sachin (in India, in the country's entire cricketing history) and Lara (post-1990 for the West Indies) have done for their respective teams is beyond belief.

We now focus on the big canvas—the World Cup. Great artists revel in painting on big canvasses. Let us look at Sachin's World Cup record in detail. Sachin's World Cup debut came in 1992, at the age of nineteen. In 1992, India won only two matches, and in those two matches the man of the match award went to Sachin. Interestingly, Lara won man of the match awards against the same opponents (Pakistan and Zimbabwe) in the 1992 World Cup! The win that Sachin inspired against Pakistan in 1992 spelt the start of an unbroken winning habit for India against Pakistan in the World Cup—four wins in four WCs. And, the last of the four was in 2003, again inspired by Sachin, with a defining 98.

In 1996, Sachin broke the record for the highest number of runs (523) in one World Cup. To say that Sachin was the backbone of India's performance will be an understatement. Let us look at his scores in this World Cup: 127 not out vs Kenya, 70 vs West Indies, 90 vs Australia, 137 vs Sri Lanka, 3 vs Zimbabwe, 31 vs Pakistan (quarterfinal) and 65 vs Sri Lanka (semifinal). Against Kenya and West Indies, Sachin was the man of the match. In the semifinal, on a crumbling pitch at Eden Gardens, Sachin's 65 was more than half the team's score of 118/8.

We will not cover in detail Sachin's 1999 World Cup campaign. Most people would say that his cricket can't be evaluated in this tournament because of his personal grief. But we will just say that he didn't play too well. And we have written about Sachin's 2007 World Cup earlier in the book.

In the 2003 World Cup, Sachin broke his own record. His 673 runs stand as a record till date. His run of scores this time round: 52 vs Netherlands, 36 vs Australia, 81 vs Zimbabwe, 152 vs Namibia, 50 vs England, 98 vs Pakistan, 97 vs Sri Lanka, 15 vs New Zealand, 83 vs Kenya (semifinal) and 4 vs Australia (final). Indeed, in 2003, Sachin was the man of the series.

Please pause for a moment here: there have been three World Cups where Sachin has played well, and in two of the three the team went to the semifinal, and in one, to the final. There are two World Cups where Sachin didn't play well and the team could not enter the semifinal. That is the kind of impact that Sachin has on the Indian team. It can be said that, without Sachin, India is an ordinary team. With Sachin, India is a world-class team, which has good chances to go to the semifinal and beyond. Even the critics have admired Sachin's record in World Cups despite his two misses—the final of 2003 and the game against Sri Lanka in 2007. His overall World Cup record is exemplary. (See Table XIV on page 119.)

Sachin has centuries or half-centuries in almost half of the matches he has played in the World Cup (17 out of 36), and has won eight man of the match awards overall. Even discounting the man of the match awards he won against Kenya (2) and Namibia, he still notches up an impressive five.

The last column (top score) is very revealing. Let's start with the Australians. Ponting and Hayden have this factor in the 15-20 per cent range. Yet, they have won three straight

Table XIV: Performances in the World Cup

Player	Matches	Average & Strike Rate	100s	50s	Man of the match	Top Score (% of matches)
Sachin Tendulkar	36	$58 \times 88 = 51$	4	13	8	44
Rahul Dravid	22	$61 \times 75 = 46$	?	6	0	18
Sourav Ganguly	21	$56 \times 78 = 44$	4	3	4	24
Viv Richards	23	$64 \times 85 = 54$	3	5	5	30
Brian Lara	34	$42 \times 86 = 36$	2	7	4	32
Ricky Ponting	39	$48 \times 81 = 39$	4	6	3	15
Matthew Hayden	22	$52 \times 93 = 48$	3	2	3	18

Note: Richards's strike rate is more impressive because he played mainly in sixty-over games.

World Cups from 1999 to 2007 (with Hayden not playing in 1999)! How? Remember the number of times the Waugh brothers, Symonds, Michael Bevan and Gilchrist have all batted and helped Australia win. (And most crucially, match-winning bowlers like Shane Warne, Glenn McGrath and Brett Lee, who could defend even small totals like tigers.) This is the context of Team Australia. The West Indians have this factor in the range of 30-32 per cent. Despite the very narrow gap in their percentages, it has to be said that Richards won two World Cups and was a finalist in a third, but Lara never made it to a final! Again, let us remember the context of their respective teams. Lara had Richie Richardson for great company, the bowling was okay after Ambrose and Walsh retired, and he was unlucky to lose in the 1996 semifinal. Richards had the dangerous quartet of fast bowlers and elite batting company! It is interesting that Richards made only 38 runs in the entire 1975 World Cup, and only five runs in the final. And Greenidge, the second-best West Indian batsman in ODIs (perhaps one of the best five one-day batsmen ever), made only 88 runs in the entire 1975 World Cup, with only 13 runs in the final. But then, the team had Lloyd (who scored a century in the final) and Kallicharan, who scored heavily.

Dravid and Ganguly perform in the range of 18 to 24 per cent—very useful but not enough to carry a team. And now, let us look at the percentage of Sachin's top score in World Cup matches: 44! Simply put, in the last two decades, without Sachin, India has been an ordinary team, with very low chances of making it to the semifinal; one more eloquent proof of this truth is that India could not even beat Zimbabwe in 1999 when Sachin had to leave for India after his father expired. Think back about the consequences of this single loss to India's chances of entering the semifinal. When it has Sachin in its ranks, India is a very good team capable of reaching the semifinal, and on one occasion, even the final.

At this point, some may think that we have ignored the second charge against Sachin—his record in ODI finals (throughout his career), which critics often complain about bitterly. They say that he has not done enough to help India win in ODI finals, while he 'gets his average higher in league matches so the stats are good'. If there is something called 'travesty of justice', this is the accusation that reeks of it. Please study the data and decide for yourself (Table XV).

Table XV: Winners, ODI Finals

Player	Overall average and strike rate in ODIs	Number of final games played	Average and strike rate	Finals won	Average and strike rate	Tons and fifties	Tournaments won
Sachin	44 × 85 = 37	38	52 × 86 = 45	15	100 × 97 = 97	5 Tons, 5 Fifties	13
Dravid	39 × 71 = 28	23	35 × 68 = 24	2	18 × 68 = 12	None	2
Ganguly	41 × 74 = 30	31	37 × 69 = 26	7	81 × 83 = 67	2 Tons, 3 fifties	6
Richards	47 × 90 = 42	18	56 × 85 = 48	12	71 × 84 = 60	1 Ton, 7 Fifties	6
Lara	40 × 80 = 32	19	28 × 72 = 20	6	60 × 84 = 50	1 Ton, 2 Fifties	5
Ponting	43 × 81 = 35	40	40 × 82 = 33	28	48 × 85 = 41	2 Tons, 6 Fifties	17
Hayden	44 × 79 = 35	17	51 × 73 = 37	10	53 × 70 = 37	1 Ton, 3 Fifties	7

Note: Number of 'Tournaments Won' is less than the number of finals because of 'best-of-three' finals.

Dravid's record is less impressive: his average and strike rate are lower in finals than overall; his team has won only two out of the twenty-three finals he has played in; and his average when the team has won in a final is eighteen! Hayden's final record is better than Dravid's but still average. Lara's and Ponting's records are okay to good, but not great. Ganguly's average and strike rates in finals are lower than his overall stats; however, his record when the team has won is great. Richards, of course, has a great record in finals, but we should also consider the fact that he played fewer matches. Sachin has similar or perhaps even a better record especially given the question that prompted this analysis: 'Has Sachin done enough to help India to win in a final?' Sachin has driven India to final wins beyond anyone in the history of ODI cricket. He has, even with an average team, led it to victories. In fact, if Sachin doesn't play a big knock, the Indian team is almost certain to lose an ODI final (the NatWest final against England in 2002 being an exception). Whereas West Indies could win a World Cup final in 1975 despite Richards's failure with the bat.

Let's look at the data of India's record in ODI finals with and without Sachin.

Table XVI: India in ODI finals with and without Sachin

ODI Finals India (1989-May 2008)	Matches	Wins	Losses	No-result	W:L
Total	45	15	25	5	0.6
With Sachin	38	15	19	4	0.79
Without Sachin	7	0	6	1	0

The table is so self-explanatory, we don't even need words to analyse what it implies. We rest our case.

In Conclusion

Sachin has transformed an average team into one capable of challenging, and sometimes beating, Australia consistently at home and away, as well as performing well in international matches across Tests and ODIs. He is the only batsman in the modern era to maintain high standards in both Tests and ODIs for nearly two decades. He is the only batsman in the modern era who had the onus of leading the team's batting thrust upon him even before he turned twenty—at which age most of the other modern greats were feeling their way around first-class cricket and trying to break in.

His critics and challengers do not fully comprehend the importance of bowling to put in perspective a batsman's achievements, nor do they understand fully the context of support batsmen. They do not understand what it means to be in a weak team. The critics need to reflect on the nature of cricket and their understanding of it. Sachin's critics do not realize that what pressure situation is to the other players is a normal innings for Sachin, especially during 1990–99 when the supporting cast was weak. This is even without considering the pressure from the fans and the media.

In summary, the presence of Sachin Tendulkar gave an average team the *belief* and its fans the *illusion* that it is a world-beating side. It is now time for the next generation of Indian cricketers to grow up from this childlike dependence on a single talismanic cricketer, approach cricket like a team game, and take accountability for their performances, if at all India is to become a consistently world-beating side in all forms of the game.

9

The Player Viewpoint

I don't think anyone, apart from Don Bradman, is in the same class as Sachin Tendulkar.

—SHANE WARNE

We now move to some non-statistical ways of looking at Sachin. We start with what Sachin's contemporaries—bowlers, batsmen and all-rounders who have played against or with Tendulkar—have said about him. Players tend to assess each other based primarily on how they did in the matches they played against or with each other. However, we must warn of an element of subjectivity which is inherent in such evaluations.

Allan Donald makes a point about consistency being the Tendulkar hallmark. He is of the opinion that consistency is what makes Tendulkar special. Donald is categorical that though Tendulkar and Lara are spoken of in the same breath, there is no ground for making comparisons primarily because 'Lara is not half as consistent as Tendulkar and lacks the discipline of the latter' (http://www.rediff.com/cricket/2002/sep/04inter2.htm).

Given that Tendulkar's greatest successes have come against a full-strength Australian side consisting of greats like Glenn McGrath, the Waugh brothers, Shane Warne and Ricky Ponting, among others, it is not surprising that some of the most lavish praise has come from Australian players. McGrath has few doubts about Tendulkar being the best. 'I have never made a secret of the fact that I rate Tendulkar the best batsman in the business.' Among all batsmen he has bowled to, he rates Tendulkar as technically the soundest. He makes a special point of Tendulkar's instinct to always dominate the bowler and says that he combines the best of the qualities of his contemporaries Steve Waugh, Brian Lara and Inzamam-ul Haq (http://www.rediff.com/cricket/2002/sep/04inter3.htm).

Ian Healy, who has had a view of Tendulkar, both on the field and from the commentator's box, says: 'Tendulkar is the most complete batsman I have stood behind. I saw the hundred in Perth on a bouncy pitch with Hughes, McDermott and Whitney gunning for him—he only had 60-odd when No. 11 came in. I've seen him against Warne too.'

The Waugh brothers, too, have only high praise for Tendulkar. While Steve Waugh has said, 'You take Don Bradman away and he is next up I reckon,' Mark Waugh comments, 'The pressure on me is nothing as compared to Sachin Tendulkar. Sachin, like God, must never fail.' Their compatriot Shane Warne is, of course, famous for admitting to having 'nightmares of Sachin just running down the wicket and belting me back over the head for six'. He, too, thinks that no one 'apart from Don Bradman is in the same class as Sachin Tendulkar'.

Comparing Lara and Tendulkar in *The Australian* (14 March 2007), Ricky Ponting rates Sachin slightly ahead 'because technically I thought he was a bit tighter, but Lara on his day is probably more damaging'. He then goes on to anoint Tendulkar as the most complete batsman he has seen.

In his autobiography, *Playing with Fire* (Penguin, UK, 2005, p. 71), Nasser Hussain writes on a tour match in India: 'A young sixteen-year-old came walking out wearing huge Gooch and Gavaskar type pads and everybody said we should watch out for him. His name was Sachin Tendulkar and even then he looked better than any of our players.'

Wasim Akram, no stranger to the unrealistic expectations of fans in the subcontinent, dwells on the Indian team's overreliance on Tendulkar, saying that with a player of his class and calibre one is bound to expect a hundred from him every time (http://www.rediff.com/cricket/2002/sep/04inter1.htm). He goes on to mention an odd benefit game or two in which he was in the same team as Tendulkar where he would rely on the maestro to win the match. 'If I felt that way during a benefit game, imagine what the expectations are when it's the real thing.' Akram's team-mate Inzamam-ul Haq has commented on Tendulkar's durability in *Dawn* (16 March 2004): 'There is no doubt he is the greatest batsman. In the last 13-14 years, he has worked so hard and has proved to the world he is outstanding and when he is playing so well, you can only wait to get his wicket.'

And what of Lara, the man most compared with Sachin? 'Sachin is a genius. I'm a mere mortal. I would like to be a lot more consistent. I would like to be a Tendulkar, or someone like that, someone who could go out in the middle and keep scoring; if he doesn't get a hundred, he gets at least 30 or 40, and scores like that. You know, it would be great to be that sort of individual.'

Rahul Dravid (Cricinfo, 10 December 2005) provides the view from the non-striker's end, considering himself 'fortunate to have the best seat in the house'. True to his thinking style, he makes a pertinent comment about numbers three and four being key positions in the batting order in Test cricket which made it important 'that the two men there have games that complement each other'. He acknowledges how Tendulkar coming in to bat allowed him 'to go about quietly doing my job at the other end'. His entry was enough 'to create a stir in the opposition, who would then focus almost entirely on getting him out'.

India's most successful captain Sourav Ganguly had the following comment to make on Sachin on 11 February 2005 in an interview which was broadcast on Aaj Tak in the programme *Saurav ka Sixer*: 'From whatever I can remember and whatever I've seen, I think Sachin will be probably the number one. Sachin has over seventy centuries to his credit in international cricket, a fact that clearly places him in the World's No. 1 spot.' On 26 November 2007, the day Sachin scored 56 not out in the Delhi Test to take India to a six-wicket win over Pakistan, overtaking Allan Border's run tally (11,174) in the process, Anil Kumble, the best and most successful Indian bowler during the Sachin era, said, 'The hunger is there as always. We started out our careers together and I have seen him grow both as a cricketer and individual. It is amazing to see the pressure he handles. Every time he goes out to bat he has to handle pressure and he has done it for the last eighteen years.' Kumble then went on to express confidence that Sachin would break every record in the book—runs, centuries, the works (http://www.rediff.com/cricket/2007/nov/26kumb.htm).

We have given you the players' views based on what they saw. Now, let us focus on one aspect of Tendulkar's career that has gone rather unnoticed.

During the 1990s (1 January 1990–31 December 1999), India played 69 Tests and 257 one-dayers. During the same period, Australia played 108 Tests and 225 one-dayers. England played 107 Tests and 135 one-dayers and West Indies 81 Tests and 195 one-dayers. We feel that driven mainly by commercial considerations, the BCCI perhaps arranged thirty-five less Test matches and about fifty more one-dayers during this decade. Our estimate is that this prioritization has cost Sachin about eleven Test centuries and 2850 Test runs, assuming that he maintained the same proficiency through these additional Tests (if they had been played) as he did for the decade (he scored 22 centuries and 5626 runs in the 69 Tests he played in that decade). What this implies is: Tendulkar might have *lost* the equivalent of four years of Test cricket while at his peak! This would have helped Sachin amass over 14,600 runs and fifty Test centuries already! During this period, Sachin played 228 ODIs, scoring 8571 runs (out of a total 16,361 to date) and 24 of his 42 centuries. Accounting for the effect of fifty less ODIs, he would probably have 14,400 ODI runs with about thirty-six ODI centuries—still way ahead of anyone else.

10

The Commentator Viewpoint

He looks upon this game as a vehicle of fulfilment, as a servant rather than a master. There is a delicious irony to it. One of the most humble devotees of the game is himself an idol to so many.

—HARSHA BHOGLE

On the subject of Sachin, no evaluation can be complete without the assessment of the commentators of the game. In the category of commentators, we also include specialist 'critics' who have never played international cricket, writers and ex-cricketers who have never played against Sachin.

Why are such commentators' viewpoints important?

One of our observations is that the view of players who have either competed against Sachin or have played with him is influenced, perhaps overly so, by how he performed in the matches they have been part of. There is a second and more important reason. Professional commentators bring to the game a historical context and an appreciation of the workings of the game that ex-cricketers, in our opinion, often do not. We have met Formula One drivers who are not familiar with the full construct of a race or the workings of an internal combustion engine. This is because winning a race—for a driver—is more about motor skills and tactical cunning than understanding how an engine is put together; to a large extent, a race is won by the backroom boys sitting in the pits who are watching the variables pertaining to a car's performance change on live monitors. It is they who have a fuller understanding of how all the various parts of the race are put together.

Cricket has a number of interrelated parts. Cricketers do not always understand how these work together—although there are many honourable exceptions. Commentating and writing on cricket is a difficult craft. It has to be learnt from scratch and the skill does not descend upon someone simply because he has played cricket at the highest level. In the earlier days of radio, we used to have 'commentators' and then 'expert commentators'. Sometimes the regular commentators used to bring the proceedings to life better than the experts.

The combination of television and ex-cricketers in the commentators' box has led to too much focus on the technical side of the game. The ambience of the game—the wit, romance, humour and space for our imagination to fill in the blanks—has been lost. Many would insist that one-dayers and 20-20 robbed Test cricket of its core viewership. We think that is only part of the problem.

Having followed cricket primarily through radio in the 1970s, we had two advantages. Firstly, we could multitask when cricket was on—read, write, eat, even study while the familiar voices of a Anant Setalvad, Alan MacGilvray or Dicky Rutnagur commentated on the game. (The previous generation would swear by John Arlott and V.M. Chakrapani.) We waited for the familiar gags—Brian Johnston and his cakes, Rutnagur begging our pardon, Bobby Talyarkhan railing against whoever he wanted to rail against. This ambience, this combination of style, individuality, historical context and, dare we say, entertainment, has been lost. Instead, we are subjected to how to reverse swing the ball, where the ball would have gone had the pad not intercepted its progress, and other such points of pure technical interest. The more accurate the technology, the less space our imagination has to enhance the proceedings on the field. And so we have had to look for other forms of entertainment—cheerleaders, circus acts and such, heralding the eventual merging of sport with the entertainment business.

Perhaps with the advent of competitive 24/7 coverage of other sports, this was inevitable to retain audience interest. But it's perhaps because of the rise of the ex-cricketer in the box that we have had to look for other forms of ambience. Perhaps the romance of Test cricket never actually existed—it was a construct of the poet-commentators and our imaginations. Perhaps Test cricket is what we see nowadays—five days in the hot sun fighting for small incremental wins in a session, which translate to a win by day four or five. We'd rather this was not true, and that the prosaic nature of the game we see today is a product of the way it is brought to us—by way of the technology and the commentating.

Andrew Sullivan pointed out in *The Times* that Friedrich Nietzsche's terse, aphoristic style came to the fore when he shifted from fountain pen to typewriter. When questioned on this, Nietzsche agreed: 'Our writing equipment takes part in the forming of our thoughts.' Imagine then the change in media from radio to visual image, and from the professional commentator to ex-cricketer. No wonder our 'formation of thoughts' about the game has changed. No doubt an earlier generation would have bemoaned the rise of radio, saying it robbed the game of true writers. Technology moves on, the game changes, we need to get with the program. There are many things we like about television—the stump-to-stump vision, the slow-motion replay and players' expressions. But there are things we miss as well—the stump-to-stump camera doesn't capture subtle changes in field placing. Focusing too much on the trees sometimes leads to the forest being lost.

Moreover, we feel that perhaps this decline of the professional commentator has also led to Sachin Tendulkar's achievements not being seen in its true historical context. So what do these professional commentators and players who have not played against Sachin think of him?

We start with Peter Roebuck who led Somerset during a difficult era. Roebuck is someone who did not leapfrog into plum commentary assignments on account of his brand name on the field. This probably helped him in the long run as he has clearly taken pains to learn his craft. The brand-name players who get an easy passage into the box are sometimes guilty of talking too much, being too partisan or in presenting opinion as if it were fact.

On 20 May 2006, Peter Roebuck wrote (http://content-uk.cricinfo.com/ci/content/story/247931.html):

> Tendulkar, too, has never had the chance to unwind. Eventually, the soul must cry enough.... Neither Lara nor Tendulkar can ever be quite the same again. Sportsmen fade away. Talent dwindles. Everything is temporary in sport. Nor will they be permitted a Tempest because sport encourages competition not contemplation. But there is no reason to regret anything. Both players have illuminated the game. And both may stir again as experience pulls its weight. Although there can be no going back, Tendulkar, especially, has more runs in him. Revival is impossible but the master of Bombay knows a thing or two, and might yet overcome the heaviness in his mind.

At a time when great ex-Test cricketers were asking Sachin Tendulkar to pack up, Roebuck appreciated the fact that Tendulkar had more runs in him. These we were to see in

2007–08. This is the difference between understanding the context of all the moving parts of the game versus just seeing the last game.

On 5 March 2008, Roebuck was to write in the *Sydney Morning Herald*, 'Over the past 15 years, cricket enthusiasts have enjoyed many delights but two stand out. Anyone able to follow the careers of Tendulkar and Shane Warne at close quarters has been privileged. They count among the most enchanting and compelling cricketers the game has seen. Both were craftsmen of high caliber but also artists of supreme talent. Warne was a mesmerising tweaker with a fiercely competitive streak. The Indian remains a classical batsman unburdened with ego and capable of exquisite strokeplay.'

Roebuck could afford to write this because, unlike some ex-cricketers who had gone to town baying for Sachin's exit in 2006, he hadn't dug a big hole for himself. This is the difference between having a historical appreciation for the game, rather than a superficial understanding based on one series or, worse still, one innings.

Richie Benaud, another individual who made it from the field to the box, and remembered he wasn't wearing his country cap when commentating on the game, placed Sachin in his all-time great XI. He had Viv Richards and Sachin Tendulkar at numbers four and five, ahead of all-time greats like Graeme Pollock, Greg Chappell, Frank Worrell and Brian Lara. In his book, *My Spin on Cricket*, he describes Sachin's 148 at Sydney in January 1992 as an innings which could not have been bettered, and also observes that Sachin is the youngest centurion in history on Australian soil, getting his hundred at 18 years 265 days. This placement within a historical context of sixty-six players, and the observation on the century in Australia, all point to a referential framework. Benaud is constantly assessing players not on the last innings, but where they stand in overall terms versus fifty years of great players he has played with and seen. This gives him a more elevated platform for assessment.

Mike Coward was to write after the Sydney Test in the 2008 series in *The Australian*:

> It has been very helpful for those who did not have the privilege of seeing Bradman to hear the little bloke, as he was so cheekily called by some of his peers—notably Bill O'Reilly and Sam Loxton—speak of Tendulkar in such glowing terms. While Bradman knew many of his records would never be equalled let alone broken, he was gracious enough to recognise the genius of a player of the modern age. After all, he played at a very different time—his career being played on 10 grounds in eight cities in Australia and England. Conversely, Tendulkar has played on 43 Test match grounds in 13 countries if you separate the sovereign nations of the Caribbean.

He was also to write:

> Tendulkar can be intense in his desire for perfection. Today, he is more the master practitioner using all his experience and guile to benefit the greater cause. And to his unbridled relief, he generally receives greater support from those around him. There was a time when he alone carried the weight of the batting. As it is, he always carries the expectation of 1.2 billion people whose passion for the game knows no bounds. To vibrant, modern India, cricket is an integral part of life and Tendulkar a living deity of the Hindu pantheon.

But these are post-facto comments. What he wrote on 24 November 2007, before the acrimonious series, probably Tendulkar's last Test series in Australia, is more interesting:

> The reception afforded Sachin Tendulkar this summer will be a measure of the maturity of the Australian cricket community. While he will reject the very notion, Tendulkar can claim to be the greatest batsman since Don Bradman and his visit this summer provides us with a priceless opportunity to pay him homage. A sustained and heart-felt farewell to him should be as much a part of the series promotion as the quest by the Australians to better their record of 16 consecutive Test match victories.

This is the difference, between having an eighteen-year perspective on a batsman versus a one-innings perspective.

Writing in the *Sydney Morning Herald* in 2003, Soumya Bhattacharya made a significant point: 'Heroes belong to adolescence. That is because wide-eyed worship belongs to adolescence. The world teaches us to be wary of idols as we grow older.' In the same article, he quotes Mike Marqusee: 'Author Mike Marqusee hinted at this phenomenon once when he wrote: "... The intensity of the Tendulkar cult is about much more than just cricket. Unwittingly and unwillingly, he has found himself at the epicentre of a rapidly evolving popular culture shaped by the intertwined growth of a consumerist middle class and an increasingly aggressive form of national identity."'

We will close with a statement of our own. To understand Tendulkar's contribution it is necessary to go beyond the views of ex-cricketers and statisticians. It will necessitate understanding the broader social, political and national context he has played in. We would like you to think independently of cricketers and commentators, and even this book, in assessing his contribution. We are after all, as mentioned earlier, only communicating facts and opinions through the written word. Hopefully we have left room for independent 'formation of thought'.

11
Beyond Cricket
The Parallel Universe of Viswanathan Anand

Batsman Sachin Tendulkar and world chess champion Viswanathan Anand have been chosen for the nation's second highest civilian award Padma Vibhushan.

—REUTERS, 25 January 2008

Many writers and commentators talk about the 'Big Three' or 'Big Four' in the current Indian cricket team. As we wrote earlier, Tendulkar cannot be compared with Dravid and Ganguly though we respect their contributions immensely. We then thought about comparing him with Gavaskar and Viswanath—call it nostalgia! We thought about Gavaskar's 96 versus Pakistan in Bangalore in 1987 (as against Tendulkar's 136 versus Pakistan in Madras in 1999) and his double century in the drawn Oval Test match against England in 1979 (as against Tendulkar's double in Sydney in 2004); and we thought about Vishy's third-innings 139 versus West Indies in Calcutta in 1974 vis-à-vis Tendulkar's third-innings 155 not out against Australia in Madras in 1998. Again, there is no comparison. The earlier generation could not compete effectively in ODIs. Some may say that this is an 'unfair' comparison because ODIs were not important in the 1970s and '80s. But that is not true: Gavaskar played in four World Cups, and India won one of these! And Richards played in the 1970s and '80s, too. Perhaps it is fair to include Gavaskar in the Test match list of greats. Ponting and Hayden from the bunch of current players, and Richards as one of the greatest, could be compared with Tendulkar in his cricketing exploits. But then one comes to the context of the team strength—Australia in the 1990s and in the present decade so far and the West Indies in Viv's era were strong teams while Sachin has been, as we keep harping, a lone ranger for a large part of his career. Perhaps it is only Lara who could be effectively compared with Sachin Tendulkar. But then, did Lara have the burden of such wild expectations from his fans?

We then realized that we probably needed to compare Tendulkar across all sports and games to truly understand what he has contributed as a player and person. We talked about Maradona in the first chapter and that is an interesting case. McEnroe could be discussed, too. No wonder that Sachin Tendulkar himself has said that these two are among his favourite sportsmen. McEnroe was Sachin's favourite during his teens. Tendulkar has said that he used to ask his dad to get him bandanas and sweat-gear for that Mac look. Maradona was a sublime genius at football, had to manage the wild expectations of his fans and his country, and had colossal mass appeal. But many controversies have affected his Godlike status. McEnroe, too, was a genius but his appeal was polarized because of his on-court behaviour and a much shorter peak. Tendulkar, in contrast, delivered in cricket like Becker in his teens (when Becker won the Wimbledon in 1985 and 1986), McEnroe in his mid-twenties (1983 and 1984) and Connors at age thirty-plus (1982), and he has been delivering for nearly two decades now. How many other sportspersons have achieved such long-term consistency? We could write about Tiger Woods, Pele and Roger Federer. But we think there is only one person who is remarkably similar to Tendulkar.

As we moved from sports to games in seeking a comparison, the parallels between Tendulkar and Viswanathan Anand finally hit us. Sometimes we miss the obvious, for we have been following Anand very closely for decades! In fact, Tendulkar and Anand are, as per our assessment, among India's five best sportspersons ever.

We all know that 1983 was the year of India's finest achievement in cricket. But very few may know that it was in 1983 that Anand came to prominence on the Indian chess scene, almost without notice or forewarning. The way a wunderkind springs up. An industrialist from Pollachi (near Coimbatore) had announced in the late 1970s that he would award Rs 100,000 (a very huge sum at that time; well, even now that sum could get you a Nano car) to the first Indian Grand Master. When Anand won the sub-junior Indian title with a score of 9/9 in 1983, some of us thought that the boy would take the Pollachi prize. And that he would go far. There was no stopping Anand after 1983. At sixteen, he won the national senior title. (At the same age, Tendulkar played for India.) At seventeen, Anand won the world junior title (under-19), the first Asian to do so. And with that, he became GM.

Even from his early years, Anand had a reputation of playing at blitzkrieg speed and was called 'The Lightning Kid'. In the same way that Tendulkar broke away from the mould of the 'classic Bombay' batsman, Anand turbocharged the slow game of chess. Anand was and still is the king of the rapid format of chess, which has now caught on. And like Anand, Tendulkar, too, has excelled in cricket's faster version, the ODIs.

Anand's first big win was in the Reggio Emilia tournament in 1991. He started brilliantly with two wins in the first two rounds, with the great Garry Kasparov being his victim in the second round. Anand won the tourney, finishing ahead of Kasparov and Anatoly Karpov. He had truly arrived in the big league. Kasparov was ranked second in the tournament, while Karpov was fourth. Boris Gelfand, who was ranked third, would, sixteen years later, give a minor headache to Anand en route to the 2007 world championship. In parallel, Tendulkar scored centuries in 1990 in England, then against Australia in Sydney and Perth in 1992.

In 1993, Kasparov (with the help of Nigel Short) split the chess world after he broke away from FIDE (Fédération Internationale des Échecs or the World Chess Federation). The causes and the consequences of this action we will cover later. But suffice it to say that, from 1993, there were two world champions—one the 'official' FIDE champ and the other the rebel champion. Most chess followers thought Kasparov was the genuine champ. Importantly for our story, after winning several rounds, Anand qualified as the challenger to Kasparov's crown in 1995. By then, he was being called 'The Tiger from Madras', much in the manner of Tendulkar's early nickname of 'Bombay Bomber'.

The World Chess Championship (WCC) between Kasparov and Anand in 1995 was held at the World Trade Center in New York. The WCC was built up as a truly momentous, top-class global sporting event—the hype, the location, the quality of the players, the prize money (the winner was to get $1.5 million, the loser $0.5 million), made it a major event. After eight draws, in the ninth game, Anand won! We can still visualize the ending: the 'connected passed pawns' on the sixth rank with the queen standing majestically to protect her pawns—oh, what a sight! The joy was short-lived; in fact, it lasted just twenty-four hours. In the tenth game, Kasparov was at his aggressive best and came up with a novelty. He moved his pieces the way a boxer would punch an opponent. Eventually, Anand lost 7.5-10.5 in the twenty-game match.

We still mourn that loss. The same way we mourn the loss in the cricket World Cup of 1996. We think that India could have made it all the way in 1996, even more so than in 2003, though we made it to the final in that particular year. We have covered Tendulkar's record in the 1996 World Cup. How would one feel having made 65 runs on his own, while the rest of the team made 53 runs in a semifinal? Ask the critics. They would probably say, 'He should have made more!'

Even before the World Chess Championship, Anand had won (in 1994) Dortmund, one of the three big tournaments in chess (Linares, often called 'The Wimbledon of Chess', and Wijk Ann Zee being the two other). Interestingly, Wijk Ann Zee used to be sponsored by Hoogoven, a steel and aluminium producing company in Holland, which then merged with British Steel to be renamed the 'Corus Group', which is why it is now called the 'Corus Tournament'. Recently, Tata Steel bought Corus. Anyway, to go back to 1995, the question was: could Anand win a major tourney after the WCC defeat? You bet! Anand won Dortmund again in 1996. In 1997, he won the Chess Oscar, a prestigious award that is won on the strength of votes from all accredited chess journalists.

Sachin Tendulkar is the epitome of the New India of the 1990s. He and his team's definitive year was 1998. That year he conquered the unbeatable Australians repeatedly—first for Bombay, then for India in the Test series, then in Sharjah, and finally in Dhaka at the ICC quarterfinals. Tendulkar made over 1000 runs against Australia in 1998, which included first-class cricket, Tests and ODIs. Given that cricket is a religion in India, what Tendulkar did in 1998 against the 'invincible' Aussies set the tone for a brave Indian team, one which believed that it could win against anyone. But, as pure sporting achievements go, what Anand accomplished in 1998 was as great. Let's list his achievements in 1998. He won Corus. He won Linares for the first time, and with that he became the first man to have won all the three majors! And he won the Chess Oscar. FIDE changed the format of the WCC in 1998. All potential challengers had to play in a knockout tournament (of seven rounds) and the winner would be the challenger to Karpov's FIDE title. Anand won this knockout tournament to emerge as the challenger. And he was ready to challenge Kasparov's rebel title, now with a much better chance to win it.

We need to dwell on the context and the history of the World Chess Championship, and the chess ratings called 'ELO', to truly understand the extraordinary nature of Anand's achievements. In becoming the undisputed King of Chess—while like Tendulkar remaining controversy-free—he was achieving not only personal milestones, but also giving a huge boost to Indian sports, not to speak of the game of chess itself.

From 1886 to 1972, only ten world chess champions had been crowned. The ELO ratings came to be adopted only in 1970. Bobby Fischer was the first undisputed king of chess in the modern era—both FIDE chess champion and ranked number one as per ELO. He defeated Boris Spassky in 1972 amidst much drama. Fischer lost the first game where he surprised all by playing d4 with white (queen pawn to two squares)—this coming from someone who had said that e4 king pawn to two squares is the 'best by test'! Then he did not land up for the second game, forfeiting it to go 0-2 down. At this time, most people thought that he would pack up and go. In fact, he could have been the champ three years earlier, but he had left the inter-zonal while leading by 2.5 points (the inter-zonal tournament picks the 'challenger' who would play against the current champ). Anyway, in that 1972 WCC, Fischer came back and won 12.5–8.5! Fischer's worth as a player, and the Fischer–Spassky WCC, made chess more popular than ever before; more importantly, Fischer broke the stranglehold of the Soviets in chess. At his peak, his ELO rating was 2781, a rating equivalent to the four-minute mile, 35 Test centuries, etc. In 1975, Fischer forfeited his title as he disagreed on many things with FIDE and never played official chess thereafter.

When Fischer refused to defend his title, Karpov, a cardholder of the communist party and FIDE's blue-eyed boy, became the champion. At that time, a player's ELO rating remained intact even if he did not play a single game in a year (unlike now, when inactivity in a whole year moves a player off the list). So, officially Fischer remained number 1 and Karpov number 2. But if we remove Fischer from the ELO list after one year of no games played as is done now, it would have made Karpov number 1. With that he could be considered the second player to be both champion and number 1, the second undisputed king of the modern era.

In 1978, Karpov's defence of his title was a tense, controversial affair against Viktor Korchnoi. From a twenty-four-game WCC, FIDE decided to change the rule to 'the first to get six wins is the winner, draws don't count'—a change that led to much pain, regret and acrimony in later years. Karpov raced to a 5-2 lead. Then, slowly, inch-by-inch, Korchnoi came back to level at 5-5. And then, at last, Karpov got a win and retained his title 6-5. In the Karpov Korchnoi title match in 1981, it was first alleged by Korchnoi that a hypnotist was sitting in one of the front rows (allegedly in the payroll of his opponent) and using 'meditative mind waves' to disturb his concentration. But let's move on from rumours to facts: Karpov won and retained his title.

Enter Kasparov, regarded as the best player ever who has played the game. Young, aggressive, arrogant and articulate (in

English, too), he seemed to be destined to win, and shake the chess world and beyond. In Orwell's year 1984, Karpov almost tamed youth, aggression and arrogance—at one point he led 5-0! Then we witnessed a titanic battle. Draw after draw, and then Kasparov won a game. Draw after draw, and then Kasparov won. And again! At 5-3, with consecutive wins by Kasparov (so the momentum was with him, and he was the younger player), the FIDE president Florencio Campomanes stopped the match, stating that the players were too tired, and that it was not good for chess (and the quality of the game), etc.

Karpov protested meekly, saying 'I was just one game away', and Kasparov went away in rage. His rage did not abate for a decade until he did something to avenge what was to him an unfair stoppage of the match. FIDE reverted to the twenty-four-game format because the 'six wins, draws don't count' format meant that a match could theoretically go on forever; when FIDE stopped the Karpov–Kasparov match, forty-seven games had been played.

In 1985, Kasparov became the thirteenth (his lucky and favourite number) world chess champion. In the return clash in 1986, Kasparov won again. In fact, the Karpov–Kasparov rivalry in the WCC is legendary: 1985 (Kasparov won the title, 13-11); 1986 (narrowly won by Kasparov, 12.5-11.5); 1987 (drawn 12-12, Kasparov retaining the title); and 1990 (again narrowly won by Kasparov, 12.5-11.5). Kasparov rose to the number one position, and became the third undisputed king of chess. He also broke the 2781 ELO barrier and later became the first player to cross 2800 ELO points.

In 1992–93, the candidates' final was on—Karpov versus Short. (From this year, players who wanted to challenge the champion had to first qualify to be a 'candidate' via a prior tournament and then compete in a sixteen-man knockout 'candidate matches' playing from the 'last sixteen' or 'pre-quarterfinal' to the final, the winner of which would be the challenger.) Kasparov was asked about who would be his challenger and what he thought about the latter's chances against him at the WCC. Pat came the reply: 'Short will play against me. And the match will be short.' He was right on both counts. Kasparov so ravaged Short that the latter was never the same player again. More importantly, with the title clash, Kasparov broke from FIDE to start the rebel WCC (with the help of Short—if Karpov had been the challenger, it is unlikely that the rebellion could have been as easy). FIDE stripped him of his title and the world championship became a divided affair in 1993. For seven years, Kasparov was numero uno and the rebel champion, while Karpov (and then others) won the official title.

In 2000, Vladimir Kramnik defeated Kasparov in the rebel championship. Anand was crowned FIDE champion the same year, beating Alexander Khalifman in the semifinal (in Delhi) and Alexei Shirov 3.5-0.5 in the six-game final (in Tehran). But, Kasparov held on to his number one ELO rating. So in the year 2000, instead of two, we had three disputed kings of chess!

Till 2000, the rebel title was considered more valuable because it was Kasparov who was the champion and importantly, he was ranked number one on ELO ratings. But the order of events in 2000 made the FIDE title more valuable than the rebel one. Why? In the rebel matches, Shirov had defeated Kramnik who went on to beat Kasparov. Kasparov went on to organize the title match against Kramnik despite Shirov winning against Kramnik. 'Who will see a Kasparov vs Shirov title match,' he said. In the FIDE WCC, Anand beat Shirov in the final—not just 'beat', he mauled Shirov. Thus Anand won a real world championship title, but as we said, there was still a rebel champ around. And Kasparov was still number one.

Perhaps his anger had abated, perhaps it was his defeat at the hands of Kramnik, or perhaps it was regret at what he did to break tradition, whatever the reason, Kasparov set about trying to reunite the chess world. To do that, he needed FIDE's help! Truth, as they say, is stranger than fiction, especially in chess. A formula was worked out via the 'Prague Agreement' by which most stakeholders in contention agreed to a reunited championship.

Kramnik played Peter Leko (the winner of the Dortmund tournament) in the 'semifinal' of one leg. It was a tense match with Leko leading with one point going into the last game. But ultimately, Kramnik won the last game and tied the match overall, which was enough for him to be the 'winner', and as per the rules, he moved up for the final showdown. But, Ruslan Ponomariov (the FIDE champion at the time, 2003), who had to play against Kasparov in the other 'semifinal', played spoilsport by making unreasonable demands for changes in the rules of the match. Neither could FIDE manage to organize a Kasparov vs Rustam Kasimdzhanov (the latter, FIDE champ in 2004) clash which was crucial to decide the second leg of the reunification process. So while Kramnik did his part and won one semifinal, FIDE could not organize the second semifinal. Thus, the concept of undisputed world champion remained unrealized. At least for some more time!

In 2005, Kasparov decided to retire. FIDE started a new WCC format, and Kramnik refused to play. His point: 'I have done my part to reunify the world championship; I played and won versus Leko. It is not my fault that FIDE could not manage the other part.' So, in 2005, we still had three disputed kings of chess!

If Anand had retired along with Kasparov in 2005, his résumé would still have been a fantastic one. But, despite bagging the world championship in 2000 and despite all his other achievements, could he be counted among one of the all-time greats? To do that and to join the short list of Fischer, Karpov and Kasparov, he needed to be the undisputed world champion and the world number one at the same time. Could he do this?

In late March 2005, he stood a pretty good chance of being the undisputed world champ. But, there was one niggle. At the Linares prize distribution ceremony, Kasparov was understandably emotional and sentimental—talking with guys he had battled for years. He joked (pointing at Anand), 'I am out now. You are now the dinosaur!' Everyone laughed. It was a joke, but it was a fact, too. Anand was thirty-five then. The earlier three undisputed kings had won the titles in their twenties. Kramnik and Veselin Topalov, who had by then risen to be a potential champion, were five years younger. And, Topalov had tied on points in Linares and had defeated Kasparov in the last round. A mere niggle or a bigger, serious issue? Age is a factor across games.

When FIDE announced the World Championship in Argentina in the second half of 2005, many experts thought that the top players wouldn't play. But except Kramnik, all others did—giving a big boost to FIDE and the chess world. Most thought that the favourites were Anand, Topalov and Leko in that order. Topalov won while Anand finished second. With

Kasparov going off the rating list, Anand had the chance to be number one but Topalov pipped him by a solitary point. At that point, Topalov was the FIDE champ and the number one player, but Kramnik was the 'rebel' champ. So, was Anand's dream to be the undisputed king of chess dead forever?

At last, the reunion happened in 2006. Unfortunately, of course, Anand was not in the title match—it had to be Topalov versus Kramnik. The whole of the chess world and fans were very happy that after thirteen years there would be an undisputed champion, and if Topalov could win, he would emerge as the undisputed king of chess, for he was the number one already as far as ELO ratings went. In the first game Kramnik won with white. In the second, Kramnik won again, that too with black! With the next two games drawn, at 1-3 down with only eight more to go, Topalov was staring down the barrel. At this time, utter chaos ensued. The Bulgarian team accused Kramnik of cheating. Each player had a private toilet. In one or two games, Kramnik went to his toilet abnormally often. The allegation was that he was helped with moves from the outside; Kramnik's defence was that he was on medication (this is well known and genuine) which required him to take a lot of water, hence the need to go to the toilet very often. Kramnik was so hurt that he told FIDE that unless he got an apology from the Bulgarian team he would not play. And in the fifth game, he did not show up at all. Another forfeiture in a world chess championship! Most of us thought that the 'reunion' was over.

How FIDE President Kirsan Ilyumzhinov managed to convince Kramnik to play again, we have no idea at all, but the game resumed. So, from 3-1, Kramnik went to 3-2, officially lodging a strong protest, which was to be resolved after the match! After two draws, Topalov won twice! The score had moved thus:

At the end of Game	2	4	5	9
Kramnik	2	3	3	4
Topalov	0	1	2	5

From being up 2-0 and 3-1 Kramnik was down 4-5. What next? He went on to win in the tenth game! The next two games were drawn. The score stood at 6-6. It was time for the tiebreaker, i.e., for four rapid chess games. First game: draw. Second: Kramnik won! Third: Topalov won! This clash had indeed all the ingredients worthy of a title match. Kramnik went on to win the fourth and last game! He thus became the undisputed chess champion of the world! Ah, but Topalov was still number one; in fact, Anand was number 2 and Kramnik was only number 3 in ELO ratings. So, we again had to wait to know who would be the fourth undisputed king of chess in the modern era (after Fischer, Karpov and Kasparov).

Let us focus on Anand now. Corus is the first big tournament of the year. Everyone waited with bated breath to see how the top three—the undisputed champion (Kramnik), the number one (Topalov), and the record holder of Corus (Anand)—would play at Corus 2007. Anand started badly. Levon Aronian, Topalov and Teimour Radjabov were joint winners; Kramnik was fourth; and sadly, Anand came fifth. Was this a bad omen, a sign of bigger failures to come?

While Anand became the World Champion in 2000—and on paper the holder of the more authentic title—we could not call him the undisputed king as a rebel champion lurked around. More importantly, he had never achieved the number one rating. The cribbers and moaners would have raised their decibel levels at the end of Corus 2007. Perhaps those were times Anand would have been relieved thinking, 'Thank God, I am not a cricketer!' For, if he were a cricketer, he would have seen heightened security for his home and 'fans' burning effigies! Meanwhile, India lost badly in the 2007 edition of the cricket World Cup, not even qualifying for the Super Eights, and as we know, critics started writing off Tendulkar.

Had Anand's dreams (and his fans') of being the number one or the undisputed chess champion turned to dust? Could he even hope to win at least one of them, let alone both? As an Indian ('choker'), as an 'old' player, as one who had been so close yet so far, what were the odds? One would think that the odds were about as similar as they were for Tendulkar resurrecting himself after World Cup 2007! But real champions rise from the ashes, just as wunderkinds rise from nowhere. We have already covered how Tendulkar played in 2007–08. Anand won the undisputed, non-controversial world chess championship and rose to the number one position later in 2007. Thus, Anand became the fourth undisputed king of chess in the modern era (after Fischer, Karpov and Kasparov).

If the parallel between Anand's success in 2007–08 and Tendulkar's success in the same period is astonishing, let us make it even more so by moving on to the next world championship match between Anand and Kramnik in October 2008; yes, the same month when India began its home Test series against Australia, possibly Tendulkar's last Test series against Australia. But that will form the coda to the book.

We have mentioned Roger Federer in the Davis Cup of 2002. Let's see what happened with Anand in a team championship. Anand is not just the best chess player India has ever produced, he is also one of the best sportsmen the country has ever seen. Although chess is primarily an individual game, it does have team championships. The best place India got in the Chess Olympiad has been the sixth position in 2004, though a sixth position in chess can be probably rated higher than in cricket because many more countries play chess. Anand was brilliant, notching up eight out of eleven points on the top board, with five wins and six draws. But what about the other three boards? Krishnan Sasikaran (who played most of the rounds) was competent on the second board, with two wins and no losses; Harikrishna Pentala's record (who played most of the rounds) on the third board was two wins and two losses; and on the last board (played by Surya Shekhar Ganguly, Abhijit Kunte and Chanda Sandipan in different rounds) India got a +2. Let's once again look at the scorecard: Anand +5 in the first board (against the toughest opponents), Sasi +2, Hari 0; and +2 on the last board (against relatively easier opponents). Now let's look at some of the opposition countries. To put it in context, Kasparov and Kramnik did not play (and when they did, typically the USSR used to win). In 2004 (when India finished sixth), Ukraine won and Russia came second. In the India versus Russia tie, Anand defeated Alexander Morozevich, 1-0. But the rest lost 0.5-2.5. India lost overall by 1.5-2.5. What happened against Ukraine? Anand drew with Vassily Ivanchuck; the rest lost 1-2. India lost the tie 1.5-2.5. What we are trying to say here is that although Anand played well, his team was not up to par; so now imagine if he had to play with, not three, but ten other team-mates like in cricket! And then add the pressures of unreal and wild expectations of a billion people!

There are a few differences between Anand and Tendulkar, but many remarkable similarities—of two Indians fighting and winning against the best (against Australia in cricket and the Russians in chess), starting off as wunderkinds to become thirty-five-year-old statesmen of the game, rising from the ashes after having been written off. To add to that: the two are known to be humble, honest and decent human beings. In the world of chess, full of controversies and disputes, Anand has always been dignified—the way Tendulkar has been in the era of match fixing and drugs in cricket. Purely in terms of achievement, we rate Anand equal to Tendulkar. But then, Tendulkar's mass appeal is immense in a sport that is religion in India.

One of the possible implications of quantum theory is that wherever there is a probability of an event occurring, the universe splits at that point and an alternative universe comes into being. So, for example, if you reach a fork in the road and you are not sure whether to turn right or left, in one of the universes, you have turned right and in the other you have turned left! It's just that in the current reality, you have made only one of the choices. There is perhaps a parallel universe where Gavaskar and Kapil Dev never played cricket for India, where the game of cricket has gone the way of hockey. And in this parallel universe, there exists a country, India, where chess, and not cricket, is the religion. (Come to think of it, we don't even have to look for a parallel universe to find this country. In our universe, in our reality, this country where chess rules is called Russia.) If we were writing this book in that parallel universe where chess is religion, this book would have been titled *If Chess Is a Religion, Anand Is God*.

12
Beyond Sport
The Deification

How easily he carries the hopes and takes responsibility for the well-being of untold millions on that impossible subcontinent.

—**GREG BAUM,**
Wisden Cricketer

In a land where cricket is a religion, Sachin Tendulkar is God.

In the 1970s and early '80s, every time the Indian cricket team batted last on the fifth day with no chances of winning and every possibility of losing, there used to be a prayer on the lips of every Indian fan: 'We can be saved only by Pauskar (the rain god) or Gavaskar.' As you can see, praying to the cricketing gods is not a new phenomenon in India. (Nor indeed in the world. During the Ashes in 2005 when England forged ahead 2–1, many fans could be seen praying for rain in the last Test. A book was published titled, *Is it Cowardly to Pray for Rain?*, a summary of *The Guardian*'s coverage of the series.)

Mark Waugh was spot on when he said, 'The pressure on me is nothing as compared to Sachin Tendulkar. Sachin, like God, must never fail.' The wild expectations of a billion people—many of whom have bought tickets to watch the match at the stadium and then the tens of millions watching on TV—are mind-boggling. Especially when you consider that cricket offers many ways for a player to embarrass himself.

In his book, *A Corner of a Foreign Field*, Ramachandra Guha estimates that when Tendulkar is batting against Pakistan, the television audience in India exceeds the population of Europe. This is the overwhelming context in which Tendulkar has been playing his cricket.

But why has he been deified in this manner when great cricketers like Sunil Gavaskar, Kapil Dev and Gundappa Viswanath were not?

Our first premise is that Sachin has been deified not only for what he has done on the field, but also for what he has not done off it.

Yes, he has got the most runs ever in international cricket, the most international centuries, etc. This is necessary for deification—but not sufficient. There have been many successful Indian cricketers before Sachin, and now every day a new star seems to rise. But these are stars, not gods. They are admired, loved, respected, never deified.

What Indian fans want to see in their heroes is a bit of self-denial. In a country of indigence, extravagance, while tolerated, is not admired. The recent IPL show marked a landmark—in the celebration of wealth. That is very unusual for India—at least for the India before the economic boom. We have seen diamond merchants from Surat travel in second-class railway compartments in Bombay, wearing dusty, old dhotis when they could have conceivably bought the whole train. Self-denial was the norm.

With Sachin, even as a sixteen-year-old with the world at his feet, you had the heart-warming sight of him shunning the bar or disco, and opting for the early morning practice routine instead. And the routine hasn't altered over the last twenty years. It is customary among Indian fans to comment on a player in decline that his 'eye is gone', 'too much booze', etc. In Sachin's case, his habit of drinking cold water in parties, and purportedly ordering milk while in a Yorkshire pub, went down very well indeed with his fans. Here, at last, was someone who could say 'no' to the perks of victory.

In Indian mythology, you frequently hear stories of ascetics and their penance, resulting in absolute power. Power through penance is a recurring theme. At some stage of this penance, attempts are made to either tempt them away from abstinence or to threaten them into giving up their penance, or both. Only the resolute overcome these temptations and threats, and go on to grasp power. Sachin's single-minded focus on cricket, to the exclusion of almost all other worldly pursuits, has led to this otherworldly interpretation of his personality. Yes, he likes the occasional car race around town or perhaps a chicken tikka masala. But these are seen as boyish indulgences, not human weaknesses.

In the case of most rising cricket stars, dalliances with Bollywood actresses or models are mandatory. It is a marriage of mutual convenience—of glamour meeting fame—so that the PR machines can get working. Here too as a matter of choice there has been no link between Sachin and the world of glamour in any way. This perceived abstinence is appreciated as Indian cricketers, like English footballers, are not normally renowned for their restraint.

He also does not go overboard with his talk. And if he does, he avoids controversial topics. This is a smart move. We Indians and by extension our celebrities are not known for reticence. TV talk shows are usually shrill and end up with highly educated people shouting their lungs off, with no one taking it very seriously. Some primetime shows of this ilk include *Match ka Mujrim* (the Biggest Culprit of the Match)—a sort of televised national lynching of the worst player of the day—and *The Big Fight*, where usually politicians, intellectuals and TV anchors have a go at each other. In other words, high volume, relentless talk is the norm. But Sachin's choice—not to get into such talks—sets him apart.

What adds to his aura is the fact that he has not forgotten his origins. At the core, he remains a middle-class, well-bred Maharashtrian boy who will call his seniors 'sir' and defer to the elderly. A number of his friends reportedly are still those from his childhood days. One curious thing we've observed is that many of his friends are the 'naughty boys' of Indian cricket—the Bhajjis and the Kamblis. Perhaps, in a life of self-denial, having a few boisterous lads around helps lift the mood.

He also owes his pan-Indian appeal to the distance he has maintained from political and religious organizations. Such associations, again very much a possibility in the glamour-driven world of Indian cricket, could have diminished his mass appeal. Whatever his beliefs, they remain within the four walls of his house. Perhaps to remain a God, you have to avoid taking sides.

He has never let fame make him a spoilt brat; despite overwhelming adulation, he remains a model of good manners and grace. There is a saying in Tamil, 'With a full vessel, one does not see a drop fall' (much better than the English proverb 'An empty vessel makes more noise'). Similarly, there is a saying in the Philippines, 'The big, full rice crop bows.' Tendulkar has never let fame muddle his head. We have heard that Sachin's parents had a full-time maid to take care of him. When he was getting married, he not only invited her to the wedding but took her to the dining table personally and served her. This, in the land of the ungrateful where maids are treated as house furniture, takes some doing.

He has never appeared to be desperate for money. This is not to say he isn't rich, in fact even now he is one of the major endorsers in India. As one of the big swing factors in TRP ratings (the combination of ODIs and Tendulkar enriched cricket boards and media companies enormously), he has benefited immensely. But he has always appeared to be focused on cricket, taking the money as a consequence, rather than playing cricket as a means to making money.

He is not perfect. The incident where he is purported to have sought tax exemption on a Ferrari car—which, to be fair, was thrust upon him—got wide mention in the papers. As did the story that he lost his rag with the Bombay Indians when they lost yet another game off the last ball in the IPL. But these stories are rare, and an overall picture of single-minded focus on cricket and rectitude is what one is left with.

Our second premise is that Sachin has forever remained a sixteen-year-old boy in people's minds. Sachin, like Becker, will always be remembered as a boy-man rather than as a senior statesman of the game. This perpetual boyhood makes him appealing even to grandmothers—in fact, Soumya Bhattacharya has commented on this aspect and a whole television advertisement was made based on the theme. We have come across a lot of people who were unhappy when he grew a beard—it is as if they want the clean-cheeked, squeaky-voiced, adolescent image to forever remain in their memories.

This mythology of perpetual youth sometimes makes it difficult for fans to accept his injuries like tendonitis. He is not allowed the latitude given to the ordinary mortal. His fans don't want him to don the elder statesman's role. Surely, he must always be sixteen and come dancing down the wicket to hit bowlers over their heads.

We never hear of people complaining why Dravid isn't playing like a twenty-four-year-old or why Kumble isn't doing so like a twenty-five-year-old. In both these cases, turning back the clock seems absurd. But time must not be allowed to flow its course in the case of Sachin. It must miraculously remain static.

In the fantasy that is Sachin Tendulkar the repeated allusions to his playing style at age sixteen, and the urging to return to it, is perhaps a plea for perpetual youth for cricket, Sachin and for the fans themselves. *Time itself should stand still.*

In the mythology of fans, the green fields are perhaps Avalon, where Boycott *still* plays for Yorkshire, where Gower *still* has baby curls, where Venkat can *still* turn the ball from well outside off to hit middle, where Kapil *still* has a million-watt smile, where Gavaskar is *still* the challenger, where Imran is *still* bowling wondrous inswingers, where Lillee is *still* stomping around waiting for the next man to come in, where Richards is *still* chewing gum, where Hadlee is *still* jinking at the top of his run up, where Viswanath is *still* square-cutting Roberts at Chepauk, and where Bedi is *still* changing patkas between sessions. And where Sachin is *still* sixteen years old.

There is an Indian mythological figure called Markandeya, an exemplary boy-sage, who was blessed to be perpetually sixteen years old by Lord Siva (in some versions of that mythology). Perhaps his fans want Sachin to be the modern-day Markandeya.

Greg Baum, a writer with the *Melbourne Age*, wrote an article on Tendulkar in the November 2003 issue of *Wisden Asia Cricket* titled, 'The Saint'. This is what the introduction to the piece had to say: 'His purity of technique and image make Tendulkar an icon with more than a touch of the divine.' We reproduce paragraphs from the article which will highlight the deification aspect we are talking of:

The two keenest appreciations of Sachin Tendulkar were made from vantage points that could not have been more opposite to each other, and together serve as an incontrovertible cross-reference to his greatness. The first was Sir Donald Bradman's famous remark to his wife during the 1996 World Cup that Tendulkar put him in mind of how he himself batted. The second is the widespread understanding in the cricket community that match-fixers will not successfully get on with their crooked business until Tendulkar is out, and an anecdotal account of how Tendulkar once unwittingly ruined a fix by batting too blissfully well.

It must be understood that neither reflection would have been made lightly. Sir Donald was not given to hyperbole or glibness, but rather was precise in everything he did and said. Nor would the fixers have bothered with throwaway lines....

How easily he carries the hopes and takes responsibility for the well-being of untold millions on that impossible subcontinent; in this, he is also divine. All eyes are upon him, day and night, but no scandal has attached itself, not in his private life nor in his cricket endeavours. Across the land, he is the little man on the big posters and hoardings, creating a kind of reverse Big Brother effect; he is not watching them, but they are watching him. Still he stands tall.

And Baum closes the article with a personal experience of the suspension of time when Sachin bats: 'Once I was on a night train winding down from Simla to Kalka that stopped halfway for refreshments at a station lit by flaming torches. On a small television screen wreathed in cigarette smoke in the corner of the dining room Tendulkar was batting in a match in Mumbai.

No one moved or spoke or looked away. The train was delayed by 20 minutes. Not until Tendulkar was out could the world resume its normal timetables and rhythms.'

That aptly summarizes the ethos of Sachin Tendulkar, the God of Indian cricket.

13
Beyond Debate

When the fireworks stopped and the smoke cleared, Sachin Tendulkar was the most successful batsman in the history of Test cricket and Australia was consigned to a long, hot afternoon in Mohali.

—CHLOE SALTAU,
18 October 2008

To understand Sachin Tendulkar's contribution to Indian cricket, one must obviously look at the history of Indian cricket before his advent. And that history, to be frank, is a rather undistinguished one.

For over sixty years, Indian cricket teams lost more matches than they won. Then for two decades, something changed. First they won as many matches as they lost. Then they won more matches than they lost. Those last two decades are those of Sachin Tendulkar.

V.S. Naipaul has described religion as being of two forms— religions of the earth and religions of the book. Religions of the earth do not have a founder who prescribed a religious creed. They are usually pantheistic as they expand to absorb other belief systems. They are also culturally flexible, absorbing the cultural icons of the era into their pantheon. Some of these icons are from popular culture, inclusive of sports, films and the music world. And some of these cultural icons perhaps deserve the absorption into the pantheon more than others.

Indian cricket mythology is vivid. We have glorious moments like Vinoo Mankad at Lord's, Budhi Kunderan against the West Indies, the unpredictability of B.S. Chandrasekhar, the off-on genius of Salim Durrani, the art of Bishen Bedi, the artistry of Gundappa Viswanath, the resoluteness of Sunil Gavaskar, the all-round greatness of Kapil Dev... These icons made the pain of regular defeats more palatable. We could at least rejoice in small victories during specific sessions of Test matches even if we could not win the entire Test.

Let us look at Indian cricket in its different eras, and see what unfolds.

Colonized Minds, Foreign Gods: 15 June 1932–15 August 1947

During this phase, we played ten Tests and lost six; of the remaining four draws, three were three-day Tests and one was a four-day Test. Deducing from the scores, one can only conclude that had these been five-day Tests our losses would have been higher. This is unsurprising. Cricket was an elite sport then, and selection was a matter of the whims of maharajahs. Moreover, there were more pressing concerns in Indian society, like independence, education and getting a 'government job'. A career in cricket carried with it only the certainty of penury at the end of the day—unless you were a maharajah's son. Ladha Ramji (brother of the great Amar Singh who took 28 wickets in 7 Tests at 30.64) was selected by the Maharajah of Porbandar to play an English club in 1926. He was initially instructed not to bowl in a manner that could cause injury. In one match when the opposition was 150 for no loss, he let one fly, felling and unfortunately killing a batsman. The maharajah (as per the 1973 edition of *The Cricketer*) banished Ramji from the kingdom and issued a shoot-at-sight order against him if he returned. Small wonder then that we produced more spinners than fast bowlers!

Losing the Way: 16 August 1947–31 December 1965

During this phase, we won ten, lost twenty-nine and drew forty-five Tests. Our away record was poor with eighteen losses, eleven draws and no wins. An early pattern of being more comfortable at home than away was being established. We lost several talented cricketers to Pakistan, as the nations divided. During the same period, Pakistan won ten (including three away Tests), lost fourteen and drew twenty-six Tests—a very respectable performance indeed. Pakistan cricket understood very early that winning was as much about bowling as it was about batting. Fazal Mahmood's performance at the Oval in 1954, where he took 12 for 99 in a twenty-four-run win over England, drove home the importance of bowling, especially the faster variety, and ever since Pakistan has produced outstanding fast bowlers. The Indian fans and establishment chose to deify batsmen, and still didn't fully grasp the need for a balanced bowling attack, and Indian cricket lost its way in the process. As a consequence, the Indian 'Oval' moment was to come nearly seventeen years after Pakistan's. We went without an away Test win for thirty-six years. These figures also indicate that Indian fans who display an excessive tendency to glorify a golden era of the past have got their facts delusionally wrong.

Brave New World—The Spin Quartet and the Little Masters: 1 January 1966–15 October 1978

During this phase, we won eighteen (nine of these away), lost thirty and drew fifteen Tests. For the first time, we had a bowling attack consistently capable of taking twenty wickets in a Test, and potent batsmen like Gavaskar and Viswanath who combined technical excellence with consistency. While we have a sentimental preference for Viswanath on account of the elegance of his strokeplay, his peerless ability to cut the ball against fast bowling and his gentlemanliness, there is no doubt in our minds that the on-field contribution of Sunil Gavaskar was greater. He carried the batting, regularly from his debut series, with an intense fighting spirit which spilled out of the field of play for a much longer period than Viswanath's virtuosity and with much greater consistency. Sunil Gavaskar was the first great discontinuity in Indian cricket—a batsman who refused to accept defeat. This intense feeling of hatred towards defeat spread to the side and India perhaps lost some opportunities to win in ensuring that it wouldn't lose. Not surprisingly then and quite appropriately, Gavaskar figures in Richie Benaud's all-time great XI. There is only one other Indian cricketer who does.

But once the spin quartet lost its verve, Sunil and Vishy, the match-winning combination, became a match-drawing one. This further lends credence to our hypothesis that winning can only be possible if your bowlers are capable of taking twenty wickets. With the same batting line-up, your win-loss ratio will change substantially with the loss of key bowlers. Sunil and Vishy walked into the pantheon, the first on substance, the latter on style as much as substance. And characters like Bedi, Erapalli Prasanna, Venkatraghavan and Chandrasekhar made Indian fans realize that winning was not a theoretical but a real possibility. During this phase, India played nine ODIs, winning two and losing seven. Since one of the victories was against East Africa, the only meaningful win was against Pakistan in Quetta.

Incidentally, in the latter match, Mohinder Amarnath was the man of the match with 2 for 38 and 51 runs—a precursor to what was to come from him in the next phase.

The World Cup Era: 16 October 1978–14 November 1989

During this phase, India won fifteen, lost twenty-four, tied one and drew sixty Tests. The combination of Gavaskar and Kapil Dev, with a steady support act, ensured that India could at least draw games and occasionally win them. Kapil Dev was the second discontinuity, an Indian bowler who wanted to bowl fast, and who genuinely did it before his knee injury. Support spinners like Dilip Doshi and Shivlal Yadav, and useful contributions from Dilip Vengsarkar, Syed Kirmani and Mohinder Amarnath, ensured that the momentum of the brave new world was not lost. However, the old weakness of focusing only on the batting continued, and Kapil did not have sufficient support except on helpful wickets, which is to say, turners at home or in conditions that enabled our bowlers to swing the ball. The victory in the World Cup in 1983 and the Benson and Hedges win in 1985 were actually miracles, coming against a trend of poor ODI performances where we won sixty-nine and lost eighty-two matches. *India Today* magazine aptly described the World Cup win as the 'Miracle at Lord's'. Indeed it was. From an ODI standpoint, these remained India's most memorable wins for a long time to come, but these also covered up for a middling overall ODI win-loss record.

Into the Light: 15 November 1989–9 May 2008

During this phase, we won fifty-one, lost forty-five and drew sixty-five Tests. Incidentally, for the first time in our cricketing history, we won more Tests than we lost. As explained earlier, this period is actually made up of two phases. One when we won mainly at home, which is up to late 2000, and then after 2000 when we won consistently both at home and away with a balanced attack and a greater depth in batting, especially away.

In the ODI arena, too, we won more matches (252) than we lost (237), with three ties and twenty-five matches without result. Sachin won the man of the match award in a staggering 52 out of the 206 victories of which he was part.

This then is also one of the legacies of Sachin Tendulkar: to reverse nearly six decades of a losing heritage into one where victory, in both Tests and ODIs, became more common than defeat. To give justice where it is due, he was assisted significantly in the first half by Kumble, Srinath and Sidhu at home, and after 2000 by Dravid, Ganguly, Laxman and Sehwag in batting, and Kumble, Harbhajan, Zaheer and the new generation of fast bowlers.

In the ODI arena, his partnership with Ganguly, who won twenty-eight man of the match awards in the same period, was to provide the foundation for the batting. Whilst we did not have a World Cup win, we had ODI series wins in Australia, Pakistan and England and a place in the finals in the World Cup 2003 and ICC Knockout 2000; in the ICC Knockout 2002, India was a joint winner with Sri Lanka.

We will now go beyond saying that Sachin Tendulkar is a match winner. We will say that he is the single greatest match winner in the history of Indian cricket. Without Sachin, the 1990s would have looked a lot more like the 1950s and '60s, i.e., Indian cricket would have gone back forty years. And it would certainly not have had the platform to achieve the kind of success it is currently enjoying. Sachin has converted the expectations of Indian fans. From people who dared not hope for victory, who were happy when we managed a draw and sad when we lost, they are now angry at anything but victory.

What Kapil and Gavaskar did was give Indians hope. What Sachin has done is to keep that hope alive through an era where Indian cricket could have collapsed and then to take it to the next level. That is why we do not accept comparisons with the likes of Ponting, Dravid and Hayden. The only comparisons that make sense are with Maradona (for the national pressure he endured) and Lara (for carrying the burden of a weak team).

At the age of sixteen, the great Sir Vivian Richards made his debut for Antigua and was given out caught for a duck. He protested, the fans stormed the field and he was given a second chance. He was then stumped for a duck. He was out in the cold for two years. We are talking here about the greatest big-match player of the 1970s and '80s. Now extrapolate the expectations of Antigua to the expectations of India. At the age of sixteen, Sachin was facing Imran, Wasim, Waqar and later Qadir in an India–Pakistan Test match. That is real pressure.

We have described Indian cricket as a religion. This is based on our own lives, and on the observations made of fan and fanatic alike. We agree with critics who say that cricket is perhaps consuming too much of the nation's time and energy. There is more to life than cricket, they say. But imagine the life of the average Indian worker who returns home and seeks redemption in that small box, which highlights the performances of the deified, if he did not have the glories of the game to fall back on? All we have captured is the cricketing contribution, but the joy and hope the game and its practitioners give to millions of people living in the drudgery of a Dickens novel—how do we capture that? There, no statistics work, no words, no pictures...

Unfairly and absurdly, a sixteen-year-old boy was asked to bear the cross of the failures and frustrations of a billion people and a dysfunctional government. We looked to him to provide us joy. Miraculously, he did.

When we see comments about the expectations from Sachin for the next World Cup or the next IPL match, we sometimes wonder how ridiculous the expectations of the fans can get. Viewed in the context of the entire history of Indian cricket, the role of Sachin was to bridge the gap in bench strength in the 1990s and take the team to the next level with a greater bench strength in the new millennium. We have no further expectations.

14

And Then There Was One

Commit all your crimes when Sachin is batting. They will go unnoticed because even the Lord is watching.

—Banner at Sydney Cricket Ground, January 2008

This manuscript was completed in May 2008 and so the data (in the book) are up to that point in time. In this chapter we cover the key highlights of Sachin's performance between June 2008 and December 2008, the cut-off date for printing. Overall, our main points stand. If anything, these are strengthened further.

There were two ODI tournaments in June–July 2008 (the Kitply Cup and the Asia Cup), in both of which Sachin was missing owing to injury. India minus Sachin duly lost in the finals. There is a Tamil saying that one realizes the real value of the shade only when one is in the sun. The amazing fact is that over the last nineteen years, if Sachin hasn't played in an ODI final, India hasn't won. And for India to win, Sachin needed to make on an average 99.9 runs at a strike rate of 97. We hope that even those who have a short memory remember the results from 2008: a) Kitply Cup and Asia Cup: Sachin didn't play and India lost in the finals; b) The last two ODI finals Sachin played: 117 not out vs Australia in Sydney (First CB series final), man of the match, India won, and 91 vs Australia in Brisbane (Second CB series final), top scorer, India won.

The Test series in Sri Lanka (July–August 2008) was a poor one for the Indian team including Sachin. The Australian tour to India immediately thereafter was a great one for India and Sachin. As was the ODI and Test series against England. This is not a coincidence. For India to win an ODI final, a Test series against major teams or a big series against Australia, a major Sachin Tendulkar contribution is needed.

Before proceeding to cover the India–Australia series at home in October–November 2008—already being spoken of as probably the most important Test series in the world of cricket over the last decade—and analysing Sachin's immeasurable contribution during the series, we feel it is necessary to provide some context. We begin with an observation regarding the importance of being Sachin when it comes to playing against the best team in the world. We have analysed India's performance against Australia between 1989 and 2008 (the span of Sachin's career so far and also the period when Australia was by far the best team in the world) in the absence of Sachin. Even taking into consideration the small base, which makes it necessary that the conclusions we draw be used with caution, the results of the analysis are revealing. During this period India played five ODI matches against Australia when Sachin was injured. We lost four of these and there was no result in one. India also played two Test matches with Sachin out of action. We lost one and drew the other. While a base of two Tests is normally considered too small to draw any significant conclusions, the context is important. We lost to Australia in Bangalore in 2004 in the first Test and drew in Madras in the second. After Sachin returned (despite not having recovered fully), we lost one (the third Test in Nagpur) and won the next (the fourth Test in Bombay). It is clear that without Sachin India has not won a single Test or ODI match versus Australia in the last nineteen years!

The next observation we have to make pertains to the infamous Sydney Test in January 2008 when India toured Australia. This was a watershed moment in India–Australia contests. Future sports historians will probably talk of two distinct eras: 'Before Sydney 2008' and 'After Sydney 2008'.

The authors are traditionalists. So we are unequivocal in our view that some of the run-ins we have witnessed—between Gautam Gambhir and Shane Watson (during the series held in India, October–November 2008) and between Harbhajan Singh and Andrew Symonds (during the series held in Australia, early 2008)—bring the game into disrepute. But the slow motion visuals of an Australian captain claiming a catch of a grassed ball ('caught' by Michael Clarke), putting his finger up, and the umpire supporting the appeal as if hypnotized, will for times to come define Indian cricket fans' perceptions of the current Australian team under Ponting. If anyone was in doubt, Ponting 'reinforced' this view with his claim of the grassed ball off Dhoni's bat and then going on to bully the press reporter who questioned him on these aspects. Before Sydney 2008, Indian cricket fans had a huge appreciation of the Baggy Green. The image of Australian cricket had been driven by the perfection of Bradman, the flair of Miller, the style of Harvey, the understatement of Benaud, the grittiness of Border, the maverick genius of Warne, the best-ever wicketkeeper-batsman in Gilchrist and the fighting spirit of Steve Waugh. Despite the troubled times with Greg Chappell as coach, many Indians would, after the 20Twenty World Cup win, agree that Chappell's philosophy of getting young blood into the team was correct even if his individual assessments of players like Ganguly was not and even if his debate on the 'senior-junior' issue was not helpful. But five days at Sydney, in particular the last day, unravelled the myth, and forever altered the perceptions of Indian cricket fans about the Australia cricket team.

The Australian team seems to have come apart after Sydney 2008. They have not won a Test match against India in six attempts after that. India won in Perth, Mohali and Nagpur while the Tests in Adelaide, Bangalore and Delhi ended in draws. This drought is the longest for Australia in the last twenty-two years; it was way back in 1986 that Australia didn't win in six straight Test matches against a particular team.

And Ponting's poor performance in India continues—he now has an average of 21 while playing against India in India. This is important because Australia–India Test matches have been the most critical test for both teams over the last dozen years. Can a batsman who has played in 12 (away) Tests and 21 innings for an average of 21 against *his key Test opponent* be counted in the same class as Tendulkar? Tendulkar has toured Australia four times and has never averaged less than 40 in a series. Lara has an average of higher than 40 in two out of four series, resulting in an overall average greater than 40 in Australia. Ponting, in comparison, has toured India five times and has never averaged more than 40 in a Test series. Part of this problem is Harbhajan against whom Ponting loses his bearings. (Interestingly enough, when Ponting, pursuing his 'horses for courses' strategy which he advocates and zealously defends, dropped Shane Watson [who had a fine tour of India] for a home Test against New Zealand in November 2008, Damien Fleming suggested [tongue firmly in cheek?] that perhaps Ponting should drop himself against India especially if Harbhajan is playing.) Australia's only Test series win in India came in 2004 when Ponting was not available for three of the four Tests; when he returned for the last Test, Australia promptly lost.

Sachin Tendulkar, who made significant runs in each of the four Tests in Australia in 2007–08 continued to do so in the series at home too—an important fifth-day, fourth-innings 49 in Bangalore, a classy 88 in Mohali (en route to surpassing Lara's record aggregate of Test runs and becoming the first batsman in cricket history to complete 12,000 Test runs), a first-day 68 (coming in at 27 for 2) and an important fifth-day 47 in Delhi, and a customary hundred (109 in Nagpur) which ensured that he kept his date with a century against Australia in every series where he has played in all Tests. Overall, his contribution was vital, helping India win the Test series 2-0 and thus regaining the Border–Gavaskar trophy.

Consistent with our view articulated in earlier chapters, while the batsmen, including Tendulkar, have made important contributions, ultimately it is bowlers who win Tests. We handsomely acknowledge the Indian bowlers—a well-balanced pace (Zaheer in the form of his life, Ishant Sharma making bunnies of batsmen like Ponting) and spin attack (Harbhajan continuing with the good run, Amit Mishra coming into his own)—for this great run against Australia post-Sydney 2008.

Sachin (rightly) rested during the first three ODIs against England at home. He opened in the fourth ODI and failed. The criticism was instant—one of the 'insights' from the commentators was that he is now older than earlier! Such is the calibre of cricket commentators and writers these days. They conveniently forgot that the last time Sachin opened in an ODI he led India to victory in the CB finals against Australia in Australia. Of course, he promptly made 50 in the next match and had a partnership of 136 (half of the target) with Sehwag in only 20 overs. We feel that when it comes to Tendulkar, it is time that journalists and armchair critics think carefully before they say anything lest they end up with their feet in their mouth!

This brings us to the two-Test series against England, played against the backdrop of the terror tragedy in Bombay. We salute

Kevin Pietersen and his team for coming to India under the circumstances and for playing well and with great spirit too!

The first Test at Madras should once and for all silence all critics of Sachin, particularly those who harp on his failure to contribute to a 'famous last innings chase' in Tests.

As India began the chase, on the fourth afternoon of a humdinger of a Test match, critics and commentators were probably sharpening their knives. The opportunity was too good to pass up—a big last innings chase on the last day on a wearing pitch. The ghosts of India's failures in the past were ripe for resurrection. Critics could point, as Kapil did, to Lord's, July 2007, when we failed to chase 380. Or they could go further back in the past to Sachin's 136 against Pakistan, at Madras in January 1999 when we fell short of the target of 271 (no matter that the rest of the team could not score the remaining 135). Then there was Harare, Zimbabwe, October 1998 (in the days when Zimbabwe still had a Test-class team) when we fell 61 runs short of the target of 235. Or the abysmal failure to get 120 runs against West Indies in March 1997 on a minefield of a pitch at Barbados (where Sachin had got 92 in the first innings). Or they could hit the rewind button really hard and go back to 1992 where India fell 38 runs short in a 372-run chase versus Australia at Adelaide. But cricket has a strange way of teaching humility to star and critic alike. The stage was set. The stakes were high. Against the backdrop of national trauma, India needed an improbable 387 to win.

Till the last session of the fourth day, England, riding on Andrew Strauss's twin centuries, had consistently kept the pressure on India. Then Sehwag went on a rampage before close of play on the fourth day to set up the match tantalizingly. Yet, when play began on the fifth day, India still needed 256.

Dravid fell early on the fifth day. But Sachin seemed to be in a different zone. Drawing on skill of a surreal level, the experience of nearly two decades, the will of a champion, he seemed to coax and cajole the breaking wicket into compliance and even the often excitable Yuvraj into calmness. Thanks to his unbeaten 103, admirably supported by Yuvraj, India managed the fourth-highest successful run chase in Test history and the highest in the subcontinent. To those screaming for a fifth-day, fourth-innings chase against a historic target, it had arrived. On cue and in style. End of debate. As some might say in Madras, khatham gatham.

Clearly Sachin loves Chepauk—this was his fifth Test century there! Three of his top ten centuries in our view (155 not out vs Australia in 1998, 136 vs Pakistan in 1999 and 103 not out vs England in 2008) have come in Chepauk. It is also of note that of the centuries he has scored in Madras, one each was in the first innings, second innings and third innings and two in the fourth innings against three different opponents (England, Australia and Pakistan).

We have talked about longevity as an important factor of greatness in earlier chapters. It is fascinating to ponder that in the nineteenth year of his career (and starting his twentieth) his performance has been no less than in some of the peak years we mentioned earlier. In 2008, he had two 150-plus scores in Sydney and Adelaide, a winning contribution in Perth, two top scores (including a century) in ODI final wins against Australia, significant contributions to the series win against Australia and finally the fourth-innings, fifth-day century in the famous Madras win.

There is a great lesson in comparing the 1999 Madras Test against Pakistan and the 2008 Madras Test against England.

In 1999, India was chasing 271, and despite Sachin's epic we lost. In 2008, India was chasing 387, a much higher target, yet we won by six wickets! Why? In the 1990s, Sachin was a 'lone ranger' while in the current decade India is a team in the true sense of the word, with each individual member putting his hand up. In 1999, Sachin made half the target required (136); but the rest could not manage to score the other half. In 2008, while Sachin was the anchor through the fifth day, others made invaluable contributions. The 'kirruku (mad) genius', as one of our friends (K.R. Venkat) fondly calls Sehwag, played a blinder on the afternoon of the fourth day in the good company of Gambhir. On the fifth day, Sachin had important partnerships with Gambhir and then with Laxman before the winning, fantastic one with Yuvraj. Cricket, ladies and gentlemen, is a team game.

It is also interesting to compare Sachin's batting attitude during the 2005 Bangalore Test against Pakistan (India chasing 383 to win in the fourth innings) and the 2008 Madras Test against England (India chasing 387 to win in the fourth innings). In his 'fall phase' he was overly defensive and that cost him and the team dear, allowing the opposition to tighten the noose. In contrast, the 'resurrected' Sachin played positively in Madras and the gain was handsome!

As an interesting aside, and given that we spoke of the Viswanathan Anand connection to Sachin, we need to bring in Anand's exploits in 2008. While Sachin blazed to ever higher glory in Australia and India, a continent away, Anand retained the World Chess Championship beating Kramnik 6.5-4.5. It is also noteworthy that the match was free of controversy, which is very rare in chess world championship title matches. The parallels between Sachin and Anand continue to grow. In 1998,

Sachin made Test runs by the hundreds against Australia, and India won the Border–Gavaskar trophy; in ODIs, he drove India to success in Sharjah. A decade later he was in the form of his life against Australia, and India won the Border–Gavaskar trophy; in ODIs, he drove India to success in the CB series in Australia. In 1998, Anand won many important tournaments. A decade later he beat Kramnik in the World Chess Championship title match. Only a couple of seasons ago, cricket critics were calling for Sachin's retirement and chess critics thought Anand was 'old'. Both champions have made their critics eat humble pie.

One last word: we have frequently come across the terminologies 'Fab Four', 'Big Three', 'Big Five', etc. to refer to the Indian batting order over the last decade. We have ourselves been guilty of using these descriptions. It is important from a historical point of view to get these definitions right. The West Indies pace quartet over a period of time dominated world cricket. But under no circumstances can one equate a Colin Croft or a Wayne Daniel with a Malcolm Marshall or a Michael Holding. So these collective descriptions end up overrating some players and underrating others.

But let us put on record our assessment after looking at the facts.

This is the greatest Indian middle order of all time. So to find words which capture them as a unit is a fair thing. It is however unfair to Sachin Tendulkar. It is perhaps more accurate to refer to the line up as SRT + 2, SRT + 3, SRT + 4 depending on whom you want to add to the mix.

The reason: Rahul Dravid has been a great Test batsman for over twelve years. Saurav Ganguly has been a great ODI batsman for over twelve years. V.V.S. Laxman has been an outstanding Test batsman especially against Australia for about ten years. Sehwag has been a brilliant Test batsman for about eight years. Sachin Tendulkar has been a great Test batsman *and* a great ODI batsman for nineteen years.

When you consider both forms of the game and the consistency over an incredible period of time, it is clear that there is only ONE.

epilogue

A Pilgrim's Progress

Sachin is giving his heart and soul for Indian cricket today. During his innings in Chennai, he took the responsibility of carrying India to victory on his shoulders. He is the God of Indian cricket.

—KRISHNAMACHARI SRIKKANTH

Every story is unique. Yet every story is repeated millions of times with some differences. Vijay Santhanam's is the story of being a fan of Sachin Tendulkar.

Vijay's Story

To talk about being a fan of Sachin, I first need to talk about cricket itself. I was introduced to cricket in 1971, at the age of six. My father and his relatives and friends were talking animatedly about India winning the series against West Indies and England, and about the great Indian spinners. They did talk about the batsmen too.

'This young boy Gavaskar is brilliant, I say!'

'One series true; let's wait and see. Viswanath is better—century on debut and the crucial fourth innings in Oval.'

That was the first time I listened to an 'Indian argument' on the game. It was to be a recurring theme. Both sides agreed that Wadekar had done so much for Indian cricket that we should always remember him with much gratitude. I heard something about 'That too away series!' I did not understand whether this meant that India normally won away or that we never won away. Honestly, I did not understand the expression 'that too' and I was too shy to ask what it meant.

Rightly, wrongly or naively, I came to the following conclusions:

(i) Even people who loved each other (especially people who loved each other) could have passionate, shrill arguments.
(ii) India seemed to be winning in a game called cricket, thanks to some 'spinners'.
(iii) Cricketers with names ending with 'kar' are great or important guys.
(iv) People remember what players have done for India and they are grateful for it.

I followed the 1972–73 England–India series in a fragmented manner by way of some radio commentary and newspaper cuttings—mainly pictures. Some of my earlier conclusions were confirmed, while others continued to confuse me; and I came to develop a new set of beliefs. I still did not understand the expression 'that too'.

(i) India seemed to be winning in a game called cricket.
(ii) Cricketers with names ending with 'kar' were definitely important guys.
(iii) The world was divided into either 'Gavaskar' fans or 'Viswanath' fans. It seemed to me that the Viswanath camp was more vociferous that year. I remember vividly a photo of Vishy (all of 5'1") being hugged by the 6'7" Tony Greig.

I also came across expressions like 'cricket is cricket', 'gentleman's game', 'sportsmanship'. I began to understand some of the rules of the game at this point. But I couldn't figure out how Viswanath was a great player if his name didn't end with 'kar'.

In 1974, the world changed. India lost a series to England 0-3. The nadir was '42 All Out' at Lord's, the last innings of the second Test. I still remember asking my neighbour about the score and she confirming repeatedly the improbable total of 42; until finally I realized that she was not pulling my leg.

Disbelief: 'Gavaskar, Engineer, Wadekar, Viswanath—all gone?'

'Gone.'

One last hope: 'Abid Ali?'

'Gone.'

Surely not: 'Patel?'

'Gone.'

Now plaintively: 'Prasanna?'

'Gone.'

In a hush: 'Bedi?'

'Gone.'

Most fans of my generation have never recovered from the scars of that innings. I still get SMS-es if India loses a few early wickets—'42' is all that the SMS says. There are two milestones we keep our fingers crossed for when India bats—26 (the all-time lowest score), and 42 (India's lowest all-time score). After that, breathing becomes easier.

With that loss, I also learnt about the unpardonable reactions of some so-called 'passionate fans' when India loses in cricket. It was my first introduction to the 'Ungrateful Indian'. There was a rumour that an idiot had called Wadekar's wife and threatened her on the telephone. Many years later, I read an article by Wadekar on 'The Two Embarrassing Moments in My Cricketing Life'. One of these was on the evening of '42 All Out' at the Indian High Commissioner's reception in London. Wadekar wrote that it was the rudest 'reception' he ever got.

The 1974–75 West Indies–India series in India was the first I understood fully and which I still remember in its entirety. Rattle off the sequence of numbers 29, 22, 32, 39, 52, 139, 97, 46, 95 and 17 to an Indian cricket fan of 1974–75 vintage, and he will know exactly what you are talking about—Viswanath's run of scores in the series. My uncle (Sambu Chithappa) worked in The Hindu group of publications and had gifted me a book on the players. It was intriguing to encounter exotic names like 'Isaac Vivian Alexander Richards', 'Clive Hubert Lloyd', 'Cuthbert Gordon Greenidge' and 'Anderson Montgomery Everton Roberts'. That was a truly great series.

At the age of ten, I started following the religion called cricket. Viswanath was the first godlike cricketer for me. Going to see his 97 not out in Chepauk, Madras, would have been like a pilgrimage. But we lived in Madurai and as a middle-class family could afford only the usual summer trip to Madras by second-class train. And those days, there was no TV. Still, the entire innings was reconstructed in my mind from fragments of conversations gathered from people who had seen that match. With every retelling, the innings became greater. Ram, my cousin, wrote about it like an 'Alwar' singing with passion about Vishnu in a temple in Tamil Nadu.

I did eventually meet Viswanath (in 2003, on the eve of the World Cup final, at a restaurant, in South Africa and again on 31 May 2008 at ITC Grand Central, Bombay, at breakfast) and shook hands and thanked him for his 97 not out.

The year 1976 witnessed another great West Indies–India series, in West Indies this time. In the third Test at Port of Spain, India made history, posting 406 for 4 in the fourth innings to record an incredible victory. Gavaskar and Viswanath, who were part of the infamous '42 All Out', both made centuries.

I read an article on the Sunny–Vishy debate many years ago. The writer concludes thus: 'The historical win in 1976 is the epitome of the Gavaskar vs. Viswanath debate among fans. On the one hand, Vishy's fans would say that where Gavaskar plodded to his century, Vishy just plundered. But on the other hand, Sunny's fans would say that only because of his century could Viswanath bat with freedom later.' In reality, Vishy hit just two boundaries more than Gavaskar, and batted just twenty-five minutes less to get his 112 as compared to Gavaskar's 102. But when you are opening in a 400-plus chase, time gets dilated. Numbed by the incredible loss, West Indies came out no-holds-barred in the last match. Many of the Indian batsmen were injured by the West Indian bowlers who let a few beamers slip out 'accidentally'. So India's second innings closed at 97 for 5 (and we lost). Anshuman Gaekwad's 81 (retired hurt) in the first innings was an act of courage as was Mohinder Amarnath's 60 in the second.

Thus, at eleven, I had graduated from my elementary school on cricket. My lessons?

Cricket is a religion. Winning and losing are part and parcel of it. The Indian team can lose any match from any situation and an Indian fan has to have the equanimity to remain sane. But while India could lose against the weakest team, it could also win against the best. '42 All Out' and '406 for 4' are both possible. One day exultation, the next day ignominy. Chepauk and Port of Spain are both temples. There are some differences between 'home' and 'away' but people tend to exaggerate the quantum of the difference. Argumentation and one-upmanship are the tenets of the cricketing religion. Cricketing gods are really not all-powerful. (I only learnt much later about Zoroaster's teaching on why God is not yet all-powerful.) Finally, an Indian cricket fan has four typical characteristics:

1. A very, very short memory;
2. A high level of passion (easily the highest across fans the world over) but a very limited perspective (possibly the lowest in the world), irrespective of whether it is a paanwalla or a member of parliament;
3. We are ungrateful as a country. In the first-ever away Test win (February 1968 in Dunedin, New Zealand), Wadekar made 80 and 71. Wadekar led India to its first series win in West Indies and then won in England in 1971. He led India to a series win at home in 1972–73. And what did he get in return in 1974, after the ignominy of the 3-0 whitewash against England? Amartya Sen has written about the argumentative Indian. A novel could be written about the ungrateful Indian cricket fan;
4. We love debates! The Argumentative Indian is there anywhere, anytime, with loads of statistics to back his premise.

The first match I watched at the grounds gave me some very valuable lessons in life. It was a Tamil Nadu–Andhra Ranji Trophy game in 1978. I watched it bunking three days of school! The match was played at the 'Forest ground', one of the three grounds in Coimbatore, on a matting wicket. The first day was washed out. Yet, in just two days, Tamil Nadu beat Andhra by an innings. Tamil Nadu batted first and the openers, V. Sivaramakrishan and V. Krishnaswami, forged a century partnership, with the latter scoring a ton. In reply, Andhra was bowled out for 29! Tamil Nadu wrapped up an innings win within two days, with Venkat getting seven wickets. I was watching from close to the boundary, behind the stumps, the best position to see the ball move on a free-ticket entry. I still remember a beautiful off-break from Venkat, which pitched near the edge of the mat, and then with a mind of its own turned and took the middle stump. The batsman walked back shaking his head. This was the off-spinning equivalent of the Shane Warne ball that got Gatting which we have mentioned in an earlier chapter. That one ball was worth bunking three days of school.

That was only the first lesson; there were more important ones. When one returned to school after an absence, one had to submit a written letter from one's parents giving reasons for the same. I requested my dad to write a letter saying that I had been unwell. He nodded, but with a strange look on his face, which I didn't think much about at the time. I took the letter happily to school, without even seeing what he had written, and gave it to my teacher, saying, 'Sir, I was unwell.' There was something strange about the teacher's reaction after he had read the letter. Here I was 'unwell' and the teacher was smiling! He then asked me to read what my dad had written. There was one sentence, which said everything: 'As a responsible father, I have carefully weighed the pros and cons and I have decided that watching Venkat bowl off-spin is more important than attending three days in school for Vijay.' I learnt the value of honesty. And I learnt that there are things beyond school (marks, marks, marks), college (marks, marks, marks), and work (promotions, promotions, promotions) in life. Each of us has a limited time; we need to use it judiciously.

I want to talk about one of the last matches I watched in a stadium. But I need to share something relevant before that. I suffered a major stroke on 29 August 2006 damaging my left brain severely. Within hours of the stroke I asked my wife, Kainaz, just one question (using sign language, for my speech was gone): 'Am I going to die?' She reassured me categorically that I would live. I showed her the thumbs-up sign (with my left hand) and 'told' her that I would fight back. One week later I asked my doctor if I could go to India in late October to watch the last league match and the knockout matches of the ICC championship. The doctor said, 'In eight weeks, you will barely be able to get up from the bed and stand on your own feet.' I 'told' him, 'You are the doctor, but the power of will is mine. By end October I will walk on my own to the stadium in Mohali and to the seat to watch India versus Australia.' All this was translated by Kainaz to the doctor. To give him (a great doctor, in fact) credit, he kept his mind open and, eventually, gave me permission to go to India in October. My cousin Jay was coming to Mohali and then to Bombay to watch the matches. A very good friend of mine, Ravi, came to Mohali all the way from Jakarta for just one match, 'just to see you regain your voice when Sachin hits his first four', he said to me. India lost the match and Sachin made only 10, but my friend from Jakarta could see me try to speak more clearly after Sachin hit a boundary.

I then suffered a seizure on 8 February 2007 and one more on 19 May 2008, when there were only ten days remaining for the IPL semifinals and the final. I went ahead with the permission of my doctor. I watched the first semifinal with my friend, Java. On 31 May, I shook hands with Vishy. I went to the second semifinal. I had bought a seat at the best stand that money could buy—beyond that, the only seats available were given to players, teams, sponsors, IPL and BCCI representatives, etc. I was standing in the queue to get to the stand. There was a set of steps—around eighteen, I think—before one could enter; at that point a hitherto disciplined, orderly queue split into eight different ones. I was reminded of going to the Ayyappa temple in Kerala with my dad. As a small boy, I did not have to walk up the eighteen-step stairs that gets you to the sanctum. I was carried by men the temple authorities arranged to have on that day, who were responsible for carrying small boys like me up the stairs. Standing in that queue to get into the stadium on 31 May 2008, I wished that I could have been helped similarly—it was tough to stand and walk with all the pushing and prodding. After three to four ticket and security checks, I got to the 'final' checkpoint. Fortunately, the queue there was disciplined. It was 7.35 p.m. The music had started, and the toss was about to take place. There were thousands still after me in the multiple queues and checkpoints. And the checker was saying constantly, 'Move fast, move fast.' Anyone who has been to the Tirupathi temple would have heard a similar expression when standing in front of the idol.

So there I was—a victim of a major stroke—in my seat, after all the struggle and sweat, expectantly waiting to watch Madras Super Kings against Kings XI Punjab, the second semifinal of the IPL. Was this plain madness or a religious fervour for cricket? You decide. I knew for sure—it was all about priorities.

Between the Tamil Nadu–Andhra Ranji match to the IPL semis and finals, I have watched matches at stadiums in five continents. I have watched Tests, ODIs and 20 20s. Being an Indian cricket fan is very, very tough. For example, I booked two packages for the 2007 World Cup a year in advance to watch three super eight matches, a semifinal and the final. I had planned the best possible initiation for my son into the religion called cricket—an India–Pakistan match in a World Cup! When I booked the package we all thought that the match would be an India–Pakistan one. But both India and Pak crashed out of the World Cup without making the super 8's. Instead we had Bangladesh playing Ireland. In any case, my son was down with fever that day and he couldn't make it to the stadium. I did not burn any effigies or damage any Indian player's home. You see, I am a real fan of cricket. I saw the match between Bangladesh and Ireland and enjoyed it.

The first time I watched Sachin at a stadium was in the India–Australia match in the 1996 World Cup at the Wankhede, Bombay. Australia had made 258. India's start was disastrous. The score was 7 for 2 after six overs with McGrath conceding just one run off three overs. But no one stirred. We all still harboured great hope because a certain Sachin Ramesh Tendulkar was batting. I was amidst the biggest turnaround I had ever seen in a cricket match. By the thirteenth over, India was 70 for 2 before Azhar went. The lion's share of the runs during the 63-run partnership came from Sachin. Azhar made 10. Sachin got his runs off bowlers like McGrath and Shane Warne. The Bombay crowd kept up a hypnotic chant—either 'Ganapathi Bappa Morya' (the favourite Hindu God of Bombay, and my personal favourite) or 'Sachin ... Sachin' (the favourite cricketing God of Bombay and India, and my personal favourite). I shall dare to go ahead and state the truth: the 'Sachin' chant could be heard more often and was louder than the one invoking the elephant-headed God. The same 'Sachin ... Sachin' chant has echoed in stadiums around the world for close to a couple of decades. If this is not religion, I don't know what else it is.

In 2003 end and early 2004, Kainaz and I were on a trip to Rajasthan for a vacation. We first visited Agra to see the Taj

Mahal, and then moved on to Jaipur. On 2 January 2004, we started from Jaipur for Nimaj, a place close to Jodhpur, mainly to visit a school owned by a very good friend of ours, Anupam. On the same day, a very important India–Australia Test match had started in Sydney. Sachin had been out of form in the series till this Test. With the series level at 1-1, the Test was critical. Added to the pressure of being out of form (and as usual, some tongues had been wagging) and the fact that it was the decisive match of the series, was also the factor that this was the farewell Test of the great Steve Waugh. In Ajmer, I followed the score; for the first time in the series, Sachin made a half century and, more importantly, was undefeated at 73 by stumps. That was the time I decided to make some moves.

Nimaj is a nice place and we were booked with a royal family. We wanted to experience a change from the normal hotel scenario. Unfortunately, the place did not have a television set; 99.94 times out of 100, I would have taken this for a rest day, but this was one of those rare 0.06 moments. You see, with Sachin batting on 73, I had a strong feeling that the next day was going to be very big, not just because of the century, which was within grasp. Never till then had Sachin completed a Test series against Australia without a century. Simply put, I felt it coming the next day. I apologized to the owner of the resort (but paid the money) and requested him to help me get a room in Umaid Bhawan Palace, Jodhpur. We managed this and moved to Jodhpur even before we unpacked.

As we checked in at Umaid Bhawan Palace, I was dreaming of the century coming the next day. We went to our room. I was sufficiently concerned to check out the available TV channels. The odds of not having a cricket channel in a five-star hotel in India were close to zero (as close to 0.06 even!), but I wanted to be sure. Believe it or not, they didn't have the channel I needed (ESPN-Star Sports). I told the hotel that I could not stay there and that I needed to try some other hotels. I called the Taj and this is how the conversation went:

I:	Hi, do you have the ESPN-Star Sports channel?
Receptionist:	Sir, do you want a room?
I:	Yes, but first I want to be sure that you have the channel.
Receptionist:	Of course!
I:	Right, I mean the channel on which I can see the live telecast of India versus Australia tomorrow.
Receptionist:	Yes.
I:	Great, I want a double room for one night. (We were going to Jaisalmer the next day.)
Receptionist:	Sorry sir, the hotel is full.

After pleading, begging and wheedling, I managed to get the only room left—the most expensive suite in the hotel (probably the only reason why it was vacant). But I was delighted! Being a marketer (i.e., a teller of truth!), I told Kainaz, 'Exactly what we needed. A suite! That means, very early tomorrow morning, you can still sleep in one room and I can watch the match on TV in the other room without disturbing you!'

Most wives would have (rightly) vented their rage at this point for the mad drive from Nimaj (where we paid for the room even without staying) to Umaid Bhawan to Taj in Jodhpur, all in one evening in the hope that Sachin would go well beyond 73. Kainaz was as calm as a monk, and at the end the day, she was happy that I would be able to see the match live the next day.

Sachin made a century the next day. Purely from a batting point of view, Laxman was sublime that day. But Sachin turned around an average series—going by his own high standards—to make 241 not out (and then 60 not out in the second innings). He adapted his batting style and, more importantly, he put India in a position where it had a great chance to win its first away series against Australia. I rate it as one of his top ten innings (across Tests and ODIs).

The last match I watched Sachin play (in a stadium) was exactly four years later—the 2008 Sydney Test, which will be remembered for many reasons. Australia had made 463 and then India had replied with 216 for 3 by stumps on day two, thanks to Laxman's brilliant century and Dravid's fighting half century. Sachin was on 9, not in the nineties or eighties or even 73 not out. Yet, all but two people I met and talked about cricket in the next seventeen hours, whether Indian or Australian, said, 'So, Sachin hundred tomorrow.' It was not a question. It was a statement. It was exactly the way Shyam and his friend in IIT answered the question, 'After Gavaskar, who?' 'Sachin Tendulkar.' That was when Sachin was thirteen. By the way, of the two exceptions, one was a man manning the car park, who said, 'Sachin is allowed to make only twenty-five runs.' He was an Australian and he knew that we were Indians (I was wearing the India team T-shirt), and he was laughing. The other was the husband of my ex-boss who insisted that he wanted Sachin to score a double, for that would make the game of cricket richer.

Thank God I was not moving from Jaipur to Ajmer to Nimaj to Jodhpur; I was very much in Sydney itself. From the first ball on 4 January, it was as if everyone (Indian or Australian) was itching to get up to applaud Sachin when he got that century. Sometimes it is worthwhile being repetitive. So I repeat that immortal phrase from Mike Coward's quote we have referred to earlier: 'I was there'—part of the crowd of 29,358, with my mother and a dear friend Amilthan next to me.

So, what do I really feel about Sachin? Rather than trying to explain the feeling, I will share something that has been important to me. Then you will understand the value of Sachin in my life. When I was trying to recover from the stroke, a number of people helped me a lot—starting with Kainaz, my mom, friends and relatives, my great doctor, nurses and therapists, not to mention the wonderful support from my company. Too many to count and name. In my hospital room, I had two precious things to inspire me: an idol of Ganapathi and a photograph of Sachin signed for me (thanks to a friend at Pepsi, Shireesh), saying 'Get well soon. Our best wishes are with you.' You decide on the inspiring value of those words for a stroke-stricken fan in hospital, given the fact that in less than three months I was walking up the steps at Mohali to watch Sachin play.

How can you measure the value of Sachin Ramesh Tendulkar?

Acknowledgements

Our sincere thanks to:

Harsha Bhogle for encouraging our endeavour, writing the foreword, putting us in touch with HarperCollins and for just being a gem;

V.K. Karthika for enthusiastically and speedily approving the manuscript (in sixteen days!) and publishing the book;

Shantanu Ray Chaudhuri for his meticulous, thorough and thoughtful editing.

From Vijay, from the bottom of my heart, thank you to:

My father Krishnaswamy Santhanam for his unbelievable encouragement to my passion for sports and games especially cricket and chess; it is even more creditable that he was a middle-class Indian bringing up his son in modest surroundings in the 1970s;

My mother Hema Santhanam for her understanding of her husband's and her son's belief (even though she may not have agreed with it!) that half-yearly exams in school are less important than learning the subtle nuances of cricket and chess;

My son Zarius for his incredible sensitivity and love (at the age of three) for his father who, he thinks, lives in the 'big plane' on weekdays and in the study at home over weekends;

My darling wife Kainaz, who has done so much for me in life that I can't even start to count so I am being specific to cricket and the book: for her total understanding of my passion for cricket in general and Sachin in particular and her immense patience and great encouragement and help on the book.

From Shyam, to:

My father Appadurai Balasubramanian, for buying me my first 'real' bat and ball when I was eight, and never saying no to my many requests for Test match tickets;

My mother, Gowri Balasubramanian, for being there when it mattered most, and allowing the transistor to be used for five days of Test match commentary instead of Vividh Bharati;

My sister, Shoba Ragunathan, for her judgement and being an effective sounding board for new ideas;

My wife, Soumya Ayer, herself a writer, for understanding how much effort it takes from idea to print;

My daughter Nandini, for teaching me that a piano can sound as sweet as the willow;

My son Vittal, who I hope will become a real cricketer and not an armchair one; and

Lastly, we acknowledge each other for being friends for almost the same duration as Sachin's career so far, leading to many robust discussions on cricket without some of which this book may not have been written.

Photograph Acknowledgements

Cover
An Indian fan, often seen in the stadium, during day two of the first Test match between India and South Africa held at M.A. Chidambaram Stadium on 27 March 2008 in Madras, India. Photo credit: Duif du Toit/Gallo Images/Getty Images.

1. *Fans and Fanatics*
A picture speaks more than a thousand words. A Sachin fan—one of, in Greg Baum's words, 'the untold millions on that impossible continent'. Photo credit: Pradeep Mandhani.

2. *The Wunderkind*
Sachin Tendulkar acknowledges the applause for his unbeaten 119 which helped India save the second Test match against England played at Old Trafford, Manchester, England, 11 August 1990. Photo credit: Ben Radford/Allsport.

3. *The Peak*
Sachin Tendulkar on his way to 155 not out during the Border-Gavaskar Trophy, 1997–98, first Test match between India and Australia held in March 1998 at the M.A. Chidambaram Stadium, Chepauk, Madras, India. Photo credit: Ben Radford/Getty Images.

4. *From Bodyline to Boringline*

Sachin Tendulkar and Nasser Hussain during the second day of the third Test match between India and England at the Chinnaswamy Stadium, Bangalore, India, 20 December 2001. Photo credit: Laurence Griffiths/Getty Images.

5. *The Fall: The Hidden Face of God*

Sachin Tendulkar walks off after his dismissal during day two of the third Test match between India and England at the Wankhede Stadium, Bombay, India, 19 March 2006. As Sachin walked back to the pavilion, a section of the crowd booed him. Photo credit: Tom Shaw/Getty Images.

6. *The Resurrection*

Sachin Tendulkar exults after reaching his century during day three of the second Test match between Australia and India at the Sydney Cricket Ground, Australia, 4 January 2004. Photo credit: Ezra Shaw/Getty Images.

7. *The Case against Sachin Tendulkar*

Nine Network Commentator Ian Chappell at the Sydney Cricket Ground on 22 January 2004. Ian Chappell's article 'Mirror, Mirror' led the plethora of opinions criticizing Tendulkar and calling for his retirement in the aftermath of India's disastrous exit from the World Cup 2007. Photo credit: Hamish Blair/Getty Images.

8. *The Case for Sachin Tendulkar*

Bowlers win Test matches. The world-beating West Indian team of the 1980s boasted of some of the most fearsome fast bowlers in the history of the game. Here, seen together (left to right) Andy Roberts, Michael Holding, Colin Croft and Joel Garner, February 1981. Photo credit: Getty Images. In contrast, the Indian team of the 1990s had very few bowlers capable of bowling out the opposition twice. Here, Sachin is seen with the spearhead of Indian bowling in the 1990s, Javagal Srinath. Photo credit: Pradeep Mandhani.

9. *The Player Viewpoint*
Sachin has been the rare player who has garnered admiration from players all over the globe, as much for his achievements as for the way he has conducted himself on and off the field. Here, he is seen with Shane Warne with whom he has had one of the most celebrated cricketing contests in the modern era. According to Peter Roebuck the two are 'among the most enchanting and compelling cricketers the game has seen'. Photo credit: Pradeep Mandhani.

10. *The Commentator Viewpoint*
Commentators and journalists have provided their own insights on Sachin Tendulkar, ranging from the eulogistic to the intensely critical. Here, the maestro is seen with one of the most respected commentators and observers of the game, Harsha Bhogle. Photo credit: Pradeep Mandhani.

11. *Beyond Cricket: The Parallel Universe of Viswanathan Anand*
Indian chess world champion Viswanathan Anand concentrates during his match against the Russian chess grandmaster Vladimir Kramnik on 17 October 2008 in Bonn, Germany. Photo credit: Patrik Stollarz/Getty Images. There are startling similarities in the career graphs of these two icons of Indian sports. Sachin Tendulkar photo credit: Pradeep Mandhani.

12. *Beyond Sport: The Deification*
Sachin has forever remained a sixteen-year-old boy in the minds of many of his fans. He is not allowed the luxury of maturing and

changing his approach to the game. He must always be sixteen and come dancing down the wicket to hit bowlers over their heads. Here, a young Sachin is seen with another stalwart of Indian cricket, Kapil Dev. Photo credit: Pradeep Mandhani.

13. *Beyond Debate*
Sachin Tendulkar being congratulated by Australian players on his world-record-breaking run during day one of the second Test match between India and Australia at the Punjab Cricket Association (PCA) stadium, Mohali, India, 13 October 2008. Sachin Tendulkar overtook Brian Lara's record of 11,174 Test runs to become the highest Test run scorer in history. Photo credit: Global Cricket Ventures/BCCI via Getty Images.

14. *And Then There Was One*
Sachin Tendulkar celebrates after scoring the winning runs and reaching his century during day five of the first Test match between India and England at the M.A. Chidambaram, Chepauk, Madras, India, 15 December 2008. Photo credit: Global Cricket Ventures/BCCI via Getty Images.

Epilogue
It has been a long journey ... Photo credit: Pradeep Mandhani.

Back cover
Photo credit: Pradeep Mandhani.

INDIAN BOOK SHELF
55, Warren St., London W1T 5NW
Ph. : (020) 7380 0622
E-mail : indbooks@aol.com